TREATING THE
BORDERLINE PATIENT

THE AUTHORS

FRANK E. YEOMANS, M.D., PH.D.
Assistant Professor of Psychiatry
Cornell University Medical College

MICHAEL A. SELZER, M.D.
Associate Professor of Psychiatry
Cornell University Medical College

JOHN F. CLARKIN, PH.D.
Professor of Clinical Psychology in Psychiatry
Cornell University Medical College

TREATING THE BORDERLINE PATIENT

A Contract-based Approach

FRANK E. YEOMANS, M.D., Ph.D

MICHAEL A. SELZER, M.D.

JOHN F. CLARKIN, Ph.D.

BasicBooks
A Division of HarperCollins*Publishers*

Library of Congress Cataloging-in-Publication Data
Yeomans, Frank, 1949–
    Treating the borderline patient: a contract-based approach/
Frank Yeomans, Michael Selzer, John F. Clarkin.
        p. cm.
    Includes bibliographical references
    ISBN 0–465–08745–0
    1. Bordeline personality disorder — Treatment.   2. Treatment
contracts (Psychotherapy)   I. Selzer, Michael A., 1934–   .
II. Clarkin, John F.   III. Title.
    [DNLM: Behavior Therapy — methods.   2. Borderline
Personality Disorder — therapy. WM   190   Y46t]
    RC569.5.B67Y46   1992
    616.85′8520651 — dc20
    DNLM/DLC
    for Library of Congress   92–52778
                                                              CIP

93 94 95 96 CC/HC 9 8 7 6 5 4 3 2 1

To Carlos A. Garay

Contents

CONTENTS

Acknowledgments

The authors are grateful to the many who have helped us in producing this book. We would first like to thank our fellows in the Borderline Psychotherapy Research Project at the New York Hospital–Cornell Medical Center, Westchester Division. Together, John Clarkin and Harold Koenigsberg lead this group, which includes Ann Appelbaum, Stephen Bauer, Lisa Gornick, Otto Kernberg, Paulina Kernberg, Lawrence Rockland, and Thomas Smith. Our book represents one facet of the research group's comprehensive approach to the psychotherapy of borderline patients and is an extension of the teaching program begun with the group's earlier book, *Psychodynamic Psychotherapy of Borderline Patients.* Our gratitude also extends to the research therapists who trained in this method and whose work provided invaluable data.

The practical work of the research group and the writing of this book are grounded on the assiduous collection and organization of data by our research assistants. Joanne Ciallella, Margaret Geehern, and Amy Vitale have vigorously attended to these tasks. During earlier phases of the project, Agnete Langagergaard, Maria Gomez-Vecslir, and Marion Zaretzky carried out important work.

The development of this book was enhanced by the careful readings and incisive suggestions provided by Carlos Garay, Lisa Gornick, Caroline Rains, Thomas Smith, Richard Munich, and Ann Appelbaum; we offer them our special thanks. Lillian Conklin was instrumental in the final stages of organizing our drafts, her skill compensating for our disorganization.

Finally, we reserve our greatest appreciation for the patients who agreed to participate in the research project. Their willingness to be studied and evaluated throughout their treatments reflects an interest in furthering the understanding of the therapeutic process. As we often remind them in treatment, they are our source of information and, ultimately, our knowledge. Our role is to help them in their efforts to transform inner confusion into an integrated understanding.

The research described in this volume received support from the Fund for Psychoanalytic Research of the American Psychoanalytic Association.

CHAPTER 1

Introduction

THE TREATMENT CONTRACT is of crucial importance in the successful treatment of patients with borderline personality disorder. Its full value as a reference point for both therapist and patient has been underappreciated not only in its use at the outset of therapy but also throughout the therapeutic process.

The need for this book became clear over a period of years when the authors taught the basic concepts of contracting in a Continuing Medical Education course at annual American Psychiatric Association conventions. Each year discussion in the course revealed more clearly both the need for therapists to master and internalize a conceptual approach to this therapy and the unending variations on the basic theme called for by the different presentations of individual patients. Therapists, believing they were being harsh and dictatorial, felt guilty about making any "demands" of their patients and often failed to appreciate the fundamental link between establishing the contract and psychodynamic principles.

Dialogue with students and colleagues made it clear that the standard of practice is very different from the approach we describe in this book. Traditional training in psychotherapy puts relatively little emphasis on establishing the treatment contract and does not pay special attention to the specific characteristics of the contract indicated in the psychotherapy of borderline patients. Most therapists are trained to take a very nondirective approach with patients, based on the understanding that they will deal with problems as they come up, rather than put them on the agenda in advance. In our experience, this traditional approach leads to difficulties in the treatment of borderline patients. These difficulties typically take the form either of treatments losing their exploratory focus on analysis of the transference or of patients dropping out of treatment. We have developed the technique described in this book to promote successful psychodynamic psychotherapy with this patient population since we feel that the immediacy of working within the transference, where thoughts, affects, and behaviors are simultaneously present and "red hot," makes this type of therapy the most promising in terms of promoting character change.

Setting up the treatment contract is not simply a technique to be mastered but involves understanding and adhering to the essence of psychodynamic psychotherapy. The contract safeguards the most fundamental tool of exploratory therapy: therapeutic neutrality, which, in turn, is the prerequisite for the analysis of the transference. The contract can be a great help to the therapist who is trying to avoid the ever-present pressure to move beyond analysis of the transference and become a player in the borderline patient's "real" world. The therapist's primary interest is to understand how the patient experiences their relationship. If therapists become active players in their patients' lives, they lose their unique position of neutral reflection and observation vis-à-vis their patients' chaotic inner world.

Many therapists work with borderline patients in supportive ways without maintaining a position of neutrality. Though such therapy may be indicated in certain cases, supportive approaches to borderline patients generally encounter three main difficulties. The first relates to the treatment goal of helping the patient transcend her* regressed position and move on to a position of independence. A psychodynamic therapy more clearly aims at that goal, exploring the patient's resistance to

---

*We will use the feminine pronoun in referring to the patient because our research has been limited to female borderline patients.

autonomy rather than becoming an auxiliary ego, as a supportive approach would tend to do.

The second difficulty, closely tied to the first, has to do with the patient's lack of any clear, consolidated sense of self, so common in borderline patients. There is a growing trend in the supportive therapy of these patients to include a "self-help" component in the treatment. While we appreciate the benefit a patient can achieve from establishing a support network of peers, this aspect of the patient's life must be carefully considered because it can lead to the development of what we might call an anaclitic identity—an externally centered structure on which the patient depends without a clear goal of relinquishment and internalization.

The third potential difficulty is the risk that supportive therapists, in their effort to achieve an alliance with the patient, will actively engage with the "healthy side" of the patient in a way that tends to push the patient's more primitive and aggressive side temporarily underground. Since those feelings are difficult to integrate into the established relationship with the therapist, their eventual emergence often leads to either ending or derailing the treatment. In other words, the therapist who, in framing the treatment, makes an overt appeal to one facet of the patient's inner world, creates a situation where it is difficult for the fragmented complexity of that world (especially the negative transference) to be successfully integrated and addressed in the treatment.

While there has recently been increasing interest in using contracts in the inpatient treatment of borderline patients (Bloom and Rosenbluth, 1989; Miller, 1990) we feel the complexity and utility of contracts in outpatient therapy needs more elaboration. This impression is based on clinical and research data we have gathered in an ongoing psychotherapy project at the Cornell University Medical College—Westchester Division. The project teaches and investigates psychodynamic psychotherapy of borderline patients based on the model described by Otto Kernberg and his colleagues (1989) in *Psychodynamic Psychotherapy of Borderline Patients,* a manual that devotes a chapter to setting up the treatment contract.

This book is an outgrowth of our experience in teaching and applying that manual and amplifies with clinical detail the contract-setting section of the manual. After beginning to use that manual as the educational core of our research project, we found in supervising the therapists that many of them continued to have problems with the establishment of the treatment contract. We began to realize that while the manual description of the concepts involved in the contract-setting phase of the treatment seemed clear, the trainees' reactions shifted between rejecting the treatment contract effort as harsh and uncaring and praising it as a balm for their anxieties. Not unlike the patients, the therapists both idealized and devalued the contract process. In either case, they did not understand and accept the treatment contract as intended, providing additional evidence of the power of the dynamic forces activated in and by the contracting process.

In reviewing audio tapes and transcripts of these contract settings, it became clear that our trainees made many procedural errors. They left parts of the content of the contract out, especially the content that referred to the therapist's responsibilities in treatment. But more often it was the process rather than the content of the contract-setting phase that was lacking. Some trainees seemed most intent on relaying the contract in a fixed way, and thus became wooden and rigid in their approach, especially in the presence of a challenging patient. Alternately, trainees avoided mentioning what was required of the patient, seeming to fear that they would come across as controlling or hostile. These trainees would state the guidelines of the contract and then proceed to undo or weaken the stipulations: "You are not to call me between sessions, but if it really gets bad, my phone number is listed." It became clear to us as we tried to give feedback to the therapy supervisors on adherence to the contract setting that we needed an explicit way of rating the adequacy of the contract setting. We devised the Contract Rating Scale (CRS; see the appendix), and began giving systematic feedback to the supervisors so that deficiencies in the contract could be remedied quickly. We also used the CRS to study research hypotheses concerning the clinical importance of the treatment contract. Our research revealed a correlation between the skill with which a therapist sets up the contract and the length of time a patient remains in treatment (see chapter 8 for details of this research).

Until now, no one book has been devoted entirely to the treatment contract with borderline patients. This manual will show the therapist how to set up and internalize the contract so that it will be available as a therapeutic tool at those times when the patient's resistance—so often a powerful force in the therapeutic process—threatens to end or derail the therapy. And, of course, borderline patients often manifest their resistance not only in passive ways but also through actions that can involve the therapist in innumerable forms of extratherapeutic and countertherapeutic complications.

In beginning to think about the therapeutic importance of the contract between therapist and patient, it is helpful to keep in mind that the salient themes in the beginning of a relationship become predictive of future themes, conflicts, and outcomes. Since psychodynamic psychotherapy is based on the exploration of a relationship as it is experienced by the patient, the early phases of the treatment with any patient are important in setting the tone, patterns, and rules, explicitly or implicitly, for the remainder of the treatment. Of course, one can always adjust rules, procedures, and roles later in the process, but the high risk of dropout with borderline patients makes such moves precarious at best.

While one could argue that treatment with any patient should begin with a general contract between therapist and patient outlining the nature of the treatment, this may be especially true of patients in individual therapy for Axis-II or character pathology. Thus, the content of this book can be applied, with the needed changes made, to other personality disorder patients. On the spectrum of personality disorders it is most relevent, in treating borderline patients, to consider the extent of antisocial and narcissistic elements that are present. Kernberg describes a progression ranging from antisocial personality to malignant narcissism to borderline/narcissistic to predominantly borderline (Kernberg, 1989.) The challenge of treating a patient is greater the closer the patient is to the antisocial end of this continuum.

In our study certain antisocial patients have undermined the treatment from the start by explicitly agreeing to certain conditions of treatment and then acting in complete disregard of these conditions. An example is a patient who agreed to stop her drug abuse and go to Narcotics Anonymous meetings and yet who continued regular recreational drug use and never attended the agreed-upon meetings. When this problem was addressed, very early in the treatment, the patient made it clear she had no serious intention of giving up the drugs. At that point the treatment was ended. The overt disregard for the conditions of treatment and the dishonesty evidenced in the meaningless agreement distinguish this case from others where drug abuse or antisocial traits were present in patients who had a commitment to treatment. Examples of the latter situation include a patient with a history of drug abuse who "slipped" but experienced remorse and appreciated the threat to treatment her behavior represented, or a patient who entered treatment while prostituting herself (without financial need) but who agreed to stop and attempt to explore the underlying issues.

Challenges presented by malignant narcissism may take longer to surface than those presented by antisocial personality. The malignant narcissist may agree to the treatment and appear to be engaged in treatment while unconsciously remaining determined ultimately to defeat the therapist in a grandiose and usually destructive triumph. In the case of both the antisocial personality and the malignant narcissist, it is essential to have a clear sense of the treatment contract.

In our first example of the antisocial patient, the first evidence of noncompliance with the contract led to a re-examination of the patient's attitude toward treatment and to the decision that this treatment was not viable without a serious commitment from her. With a malignant narcissist, the contract is essential as a provider of bearings for the methods and goals of treatment. When any sign of the patient's underlying triumphant agenda becomes apparent, the therapist can refer back to the contract and wonder with the patient about the meaning of her current grandiose and adversarial behavior in relation to the understanding established in the contract.

In general, the challenging and resistant nature of Borderline Personality Disorder (BPD) suggests that a treatment contract at the onset is indispensable. In addition to setting the conditions and tone of the therapy, the contract serves to address the question of the *limitations* of therapy. This is essential in patients whose inner world includes object representations characterized by omnipotence and whose preoedipal needs are experienced so intensely.

Borderline Pathology and Its Relation to the Treatment Contract

It is important to be clear about the definition of borderline pathology and the description of patients with whom our approach has been tried. The patients in our clinical research were diagnosed as having BPD according to the eight criteria of DSM-III-R, Axis II. We used these criteria because of their reliable assessment and common usage, which enable us to relate our clinical experience to that of others.

The eight criteria for BPD in Axis II cover areas of explicit behavior (impulsivity in two or more areas, suicidal thoughts or behavior), affective disregulation (inappropriate expression of anger, labile moods, unstable interpersonal relations), and identity difficulties (identity diffusion, feelings of emptiness and boredom, frantic efforts to avoid real or imagined abandonment). Clearly, because many of these characteristics can lead to difficulties in beginning and staying in treatment, explicit attention must be paid to them in setting up the conditions of treatment, or contracting.

It is also true that patients can be diagnosed as BPD with many different combinations of the diagnostic criteria. One patient may present with especially strong identity issues and difficulty being alone; another's most serious problems may be with impulsivity; a third may have most trouble with affective lability; yet another might experience intense difficulties in all of these areas. The variability in clinical presentations possible within this diagnostic category is one reason that the contract-setting process is not simply a rubber stamp across all borderline patients but includes both standard elements and elements that are tailored to the specific individual's presentation and history.

The main authors on borderline personality have proposed differing conceptualizations of the pathology and how to treat it. Views on etiology either emphasize developmental factors (Masterson, 1972; Buie & Adler, 1982; Volkan, 1987) or an interaction of constitutional and developmental factors (Kernberg, 1975; Gunderson, 1984; Linehan, 1987; Stone, 1990). The pathology is alternatively considered one organized around deficit (Giovacchini, 1979; Buie & Adler, 1982; Linehan, 1987), conflict (Kernberg, 1975; Masterson & Rinsley, 1975), or a combination of the two (Gunderson, 1984). Proposed treatments either favor supportive techniques (Giovacchini, 1979; Buie & Adler, 1982; Chessick, 1979; Linehan, 1987), expressive ones (Kernberg, 1984; Masterson, 1976), or a mixed approach (Gunderson, 1984). While their positions on such issues may differ, these authors agree on the need for special attention in therapy to the stability of the treatment frame (Waldinger & Gunderson, 1987) as dictated by the characteristics of the syndrome. It is this need we are addressing in the current volume.

The tendency of the borderline patient to act out rather than experience feelings bodes against successful treatment for two reasons: first, discharging uncomfortable feelings through actions rather than exploring them through words runs counter to the essence of psychodynamic therapy; and second, acting-out and self-destructive behaviors may threaten continued participation in treatment. A classic example of the impact of acting out is when the patient's suicidal actions lead the therapist to assume the role of lifeguard and abandon that of exploratory therapist.

The affective disregulation, anger, and unstable relations that characterize borderline patients are manifested in the relationship with the therapist. While this experience provides essential first-hand material for the therapist, if not handled skillfully it can also threaten the smooth continuation of the treatment. For example, patients may repeatedly call their therapists at home with angry or desperate messages, intruding on their personal life to the point that the therapists have great difficulty maintaining a neutral listening stance in session.

While DSM-III-R defines BPD from a set of behaviors that can be reliably assessed, there are other approaches to conceptualizing borderline pathology, such as the structural point of view of Kernberg. From this perspective, it is not so much the behaviors of the moment that are important, but rather the underlying structure of the personality. Borderline personality organization (BPO) (Kernberg, 1975) is a broader concept than the borderline personality disorder of DSM-III-R, in that all BPD patients will have BPO but not vice versa.

BPO is characterized by the use of primitive defense mechanisms, variable reality testing, and identity diffusion. One must envision the process with which such a patient would approach a treatment and its contract. The defense mechanisms of splitting, projective identification, denial, omnipotence, and idealization/devaluation create havoc in any relationship, the therapeutic relationship being no exception. For example, these defense mechanisms can complicate treatment in situations where patients, via projective identification, induce a sense of guilt in their therapists, leading the latter to question if they are doing enough for their patients and to consider abandoning their exploratory stance in favor of a more actively supportive one. An internalized grasp of the contract would alert the therapists to examine what is going on in the treatment before making any changes in method and ideally would lead to an interpretation of the projective process taking place.

The borderline patient's intermittent lapses in reality testing create special challenges for the therapist, especially in the form of transference psychoses based on a fixed distortion of the representation of the therapist in the patient's mind. The patient's identity diffusion and the concomitant sense of inner emptiness often lead either to attempts to turn the therapeutic relationship into a "real," gratifying relationship or to flee from the treatment when acting-out avoidant behaviors have been contained and the sense of inner emptiness is experienced more directly. Attempting to make the relationship with the therapist "real," for example, one patient began to spy on her therapist and his family, hoping to realize her wish that they become a surrogate family for her. At that point, the exploratory work in sessions was merely a pretext for the patient's plan to insert herself into the therapist's family. When the therapist addressed this behavior, referring back to the roles of patient and therapist as defined by the contract, the patient acknowledged the countertherapeutic effect of her actions and began to explore the profound affects underlying those behaviors.

Our description of borderline pathology elucidates how certain aspects of the pathology and certain behaviors may have the impact of threatening or sabotaging the therapy. Clinicians sometimes refer to "the patient sabotaging the treatment," but, except in the case of the most clear-cut antisocial patient, it is more accurate to acknowledge the complexity of the psychic reality and to see the threat as coming from an unintegrated facet of the patient's inner world or as the outcome of conflict within that world, rather than as the patient's conscious intention.

In addition, what is the therapist's responsibility in these matters? Therapists who believe that, with enough effort, they can make every patient stay the course are engaging in omnipotence; those who feel that they have done their job simply by offering the treatment without gearing it to the individual patient's pathology are victims of their own grandiosity. Reasonable therapists reside between these poles. They recognize that only by analyzing that *part* of their patients that wishes to sabotage the treatment can the patients' most self-destructive and life-limiting issues be encountered and ultimately resolved. However, to do this, therapists must do what they can to elicit their patients' cooperation in anticipating that the patients will experience a need to convert the wish into the deed. In many cases, the preliminary work of contracting, and subsequent reference to it, will make the analysis possible.

Because of the nature of their pathology, the dropout rate from therapy is higher for borderline patients than for other diagnostic groups; we will review this literature in some detail in chapter 8. One of our main goals in this book is to teach the therapist how to tailor treatment to the patient's pathology so as to help the patient remain in treatment. The second main goal is to teach therapists to understand the role of the contract in helping them stay on course throughout a therapy that will inevitably include strong disruptive pressures to abandon the exploratory task of psychodynamic therapy.

The Plan of the Book

Chapter 2 of this book discusses the concept of the treatment contract in psychotherapy in general and then elaborates on the very specific nature and functions of the contract in psychodynamic psychotherapy with borderline patients. We compare the contract in this type of therapy first with the contract as taught in the manual for Interpersonal Therapy (IPT), a therapy based on psychodynamic concepts that targets a depressed population, and then with the contract that is used in Dialectic Behavioral Therapy (DBT), a cognitive-behavioral treatment directed at a borderline population.

Chapter 3 reviews those areas the therapist must cover when setting up the treatment contract, both in terms of the universal conditions of treatment that apply in all cases of psychodynamic therapy with borderline patients and also in terms of what individual areas the therapist must decide to address with a given patient based on her specific history. This chapter includes a sample contract-setting session with a running commentary.

Chapter 4 picks up on the principles and techniques of contract setting that have been illustrated and discusses common ways in which the dynamics of the interaction with a borderline patient tend to interfere with the therapist's efforts to work out a satisfactory understanding with the patient about the conditions of treatment. Chapter 5 is based on the specific questions our students and supervisees bring to us most frequently. These questions are based on the ways in which specific patients have undermined the therapeutic process in prior treatments and on the therapists' efforts to devise a frame for the treatment that will best contain the patient's acting out of her resistance so that it can be observed and analyzed. This part of the treatment-contracting process tests the therapists' ability to use their understanding of the principles of contracting in a creative way to address their patient's specific presentation and history.

We have found in our teaching and supervision that therapists learning this method often err in characteristic ways. Therefore, chapter 6 presents and comments on two contract-setting sessions which are examples of very different, but typical, ways in which therapists lose touch with the conceptual underpinnings of the contract and get caught up in countertherapeutic interactions as they attempt to establish the frame within which the treatment will take place.

Chapter 7 follows one case over a two-year period, sampling specific sessions while focusing on the ongoing role of the treatment contract throughout the therapy. We show how the therapist can continue to refer to the structure of treatment agreed to in the contract as a means of advancing the therapeutic dialogue and understanding. Chapter 8, the final chapter of the book, presents research on factors related to the high incidence of therapies with borderline patients that end in dropout. Results of this research provide evidence that a well-established treatment contract is associated with a lower likelihood that a patient will drop out of treatment.

The case material in this book is based on clinical work within the context of a psychotherapy research project. Names, identifying characteristics, and other details of the cases have been changed to protect confidentiality, without sacrificing the clinical and educational value of the material.

CHAPTER 2

The Treatment Contract: Its Function in Therapy

The Contract in Dynamic Therapies

PSYCHODYNAMIC PSYCHOTHERAPY

The defining characteristic of psychodynamic psychotherapy is the exploration of the borderline patient's inner world, with its primitive self- and other-representations, and of the conflicts and affects that arise when these unrealistic part-object representations clash, either within the patient's psyche or in the interface between the patient's inner world and external reality. Because it seeks to achieve understanding through verbal exchange, the therapy does not call for the therapist's involvement in the practical concerns of the patient's life. Rather, it is based on the psychoanalytic understanding of the transference, which recognizes that the internal templates governing the patient's experience of herself and of the world around her will emerge and become available to analysis in a setting of therapeutic neutrality.

The psychodynamic therapy of a borderline patient must address those specific aspects of the pathology that so often lead to treatment failure either by dropout or by collusion between therapist and patient around the resistance. To address these issues, the therapist begins by setting up a frame for the treatment that will protect the psychodynamic work from the alternating entreaties and aggression of the patient. The therapist underlines the importance of this frame by emphasizing to the patient that therapy does not begin until there is a mutual agreement between therapist and patient regarding the conditions of treatment. The establishment of this agreement is the contract setting.

The treatment contract is defined variously by clinical writers, and diverse elements are referred to even when there is some commonality in their definitions. We employ the term "contract" here because it is widely used and understood. Yet the term has connotations that are unfortunate when applied to psychodynamic psychotherapy—connotations of rigidity, preoccupation with detail, and the need to clarify all ambiguity before proceeding with the work. A more appropriate word might be "compact," which implies a general agreement in principle and a mutual understanding of the project to be embarked upon without suggesting a literal-mindedness about each detail that would be incompatible with the nature of the endeavor—which must accept and address all the ambiguities, complexities, and contradictions inherent in the psyche. But after having considered the pejorative connotations of "contract," we decided nonetheless to continue to use the term. Like "confrontation," it has been accorded an established place in the literature despite being burdened with certain inexact connotations.

In our work, we consider a treatment contract to be a verbal understanding and agreement reached between therapist and patient at the beginning of treatment (in the pre-therapy phase). It specifies the nature of the therapy the participants are considering and addresses predictable threats that the patient's pathology may present to the treatment process. Discussion of the treatment includes the goals of therapy, the methods to be used in pursuing them, the role of each participant, the responsibilities of the participants to each other and to the treatment, and the limits of their responsibilities. The contract makes it clear that the treatment and the therapist have limits; it specifies what they can offer and what they cannot offer. Our position is that such an agreement must be in place before an exploratory therapy can proceed.

Earlier authors have discussed other reasons for introducing structure at the beginning of treatment. Their motivations include: 1) shortening the length of treatment and agreeing upon a brief therapy; 2) inducting lower-class patients into a therapy that is seen as an alien discourse to them; 3) reducing the number of premature dropouts; and 4) equalizing the social status of patient and therapist so that both know what to expect from their work together. Our own motivation, as the reader will discern, is related to, but not totally captured by, these goals. In our work with the contract, we have narrowed our focus to its specific role in psychodynamic psychotherapy with borderline patients.

BEGINNING PSYCHODYNAMIC THERAPY

In his seminal work, *Character Analysis* (1949), Wilhelm Reich described the importance of the beginning phase of working with a patient:

> . . . the preparations for a voyage, to which Freud likened an analysis, have much to do with the voyage itself and may decide its success or failure. In analysis, at any rate, everything depends on how it is started. A case which has been started in a wrong or confused manner is usually lost. Most cases present the greatest difficulties in the introductory period, no matter whether they "go well" or not. It is precisely the cases which seemingly go smoothly in the beginning who [sic] later present the greatest difficulties, because the smooth course in the beginning makes difficult the early recognition and elimination of the difficulties. (p. 20)

Paul Dewald (1969) provides a comprehensive discussion of the issues to be considered in the process of setting up the frame, emphasizing that "the details of the structuring of the therapeutic situation and agreement should vary as a function of the total therapeutic strategy" (p. 161). Robert Langs (1976; Langs and Stone, 1980) also stresses the importance of the frame in the therapeutic situation, especially in terms of the significance that any alterations in the frame may have on the process of therapy.

Given the necessity of a frame of treatment in the dynamic process, one might ask if setting the treatment contract with borderline patients differs in any way from what is done with other types of patients. In chapter 1 we have argued that the nature of borderline pathology calls for special attention to the contract and necessitates certain modifica-

14

tions in setting it up. The borderline patient's primitive defense mechanisms, impulsive and self-destructive behaviors (including undermining previous treatments), and abrupt shifts of mood and attitude all need to be addressed in the contract setting. An essential part of the contracting process with borderline patients, which we shall elaborate on later, is soliciting the patient's reaction to the proposed conditions of treatment. This process serves a number of purposes. First, it emphasizes to the patient that her input is essential to the treatment and that her participation is voluntary. Making this clear at the beginning of treatment creates a reference point for the therapist to use if the patient, at a later time, distorts the therapeutic situation and presents it as an arrangement in which she participates only by force. Soliciting the patient's reaction to the proposed treatment also helps the therapist learn how the patient contributes to and experiences interactions.

Our regard for the contract in working with the borderline patient stems from our impression that patients characteristically tend to undo the conditions of treatment, thus making this special emphasis necessary. Undoing the treatment is a very active form of the phenomenon of resistance. While resistance is an element in any psychodynamic psychotherapy, it can be an especially strong force in borderline patients. Our emphasis on *working with* resistance in these patients separates us from those writers who use a more cognitive approach in treating borderline pathology (for example, Linehan, 1987) and who do not see the resistance as either an ongoing threat to be contended with or a potentially rich source of therapeutic understanding.

The contract also predicts and addresses what kinds of attack the treatment might be subjected to when the aggressive drives of the borderline patient are directed at the therapy. Therefore, another characteristic of contracts with borderline patients, which we will elaborate on in chapters 3 and 5, is that they are based on the patient's specific past experience. In evaluating the patient, before beginning the contracting process, the therapist specifically elicits those past behaviors associated with prior treatment failure. The therapist then takes these behaviors into account when formulating the conditions of treatment that will apply if the patient enters therapy. Thus, the therapist informs the patient that her past behavior is the best predictor of the future, and that treating her as responsible for her past ensures that she will be taken seriously in the present.

15

It should be clear by now that the evaluation and contract-setting process is a way for therapists to gain important data to include in their understanding of the patient. This process is also the patient's first exposure to the therapist, to what he or she considers important, and to how he or she is likely to view the patient and her contribution throughout the treatment. These initial impressions are important in helping the patient decide whether she is interested in pursuing this form of treatment. For both therapist and patient the initial impressions from the interactions in the contract setting have lasting significance.

The contract is the first collaborative effort between patient and therapist and, as such, is the blueprint for the efforts that follow. It is, therefore, important to understand the contract setting as a dialogue—a process in which each participant has an active and responsible role. The treatment contract is often misunderstood as a simple, unilateral proclamation made by the therapist at the beginning of treatment. In this view, two parties have implicitly agreed to begin therapy, whereupon the therapist states the rules, which the patient presumably hears, understands, and accepts. This version of the process, however, invites difficulties later in treatment. A patient who has not actively participated in the contract setting may avoid responsibility for the therapy by claiming either that she submitted to a treatment forced on her by the therapist and/or that she has the right to passively expect that the therapy, and the therapist who imposed it, will make her better. In effect, a unilateral contract is simply the initial step in a noncollaborative treatment.

To prevent this from occurring, a guiding principle with borderline patients is that the therapy should not begin until the contract has been fully discussed and both parties have clearly participated in its creation. Nothing is as binding as what one has been involved in creating. Any contact between potential therapist and potential patient before this mutual agreement has been made is consultation, not therapy—even if discussing the contract continues for a number of sessions beyond the history-taking evaluation. This sequence should be adhered to, notwithstanding the fact that borderline patients often come to therapists in crisis asking for immediate help, both because it is their way of life and because they wish to avoid acknowledging the work necessary to effect change. Magic and contracts are antithetical to one another.

16

Functions of the Contract

The course of the contracting process is determined by the many functions the contract serves in specifying a therapy geared to borderline pathology. These functions are described in table 2.1.

DEFINING RESPONSIBILITY IN THE THERAPY

The contract is established to define the therapy as an endeavor in which each person has work and responsibilities; it is not a prescription in which the patient can assume a passive role, expecting to be made better by the therapist. The process of contract setting carried out as a dialogue both describes this mutual responsibility and provides an *in vivo* demonstration of it. This demonstration may be especially helpful to the type of patient who begins therapy with a statement, explicit or

TABLE 2.1

Contract Functions

I. Defining responsibility in the therapy
II. Protecting the therapy; allowing therapy — as a joint effort towards understanding — to happen; containing the patient's dynamics so that they can be observed and understood rather than acted upon
   A. Containing the patient's aggression and seduction
   B. Creating conditions of work that allow the therapist to feel safe, to maintain neutrality, and to think and reflect clearly
   C. Creating a safe place for the patient's dynamics and affects to unfold
III. Instructing the patient
   A. Describing the patient role; defining therapy as talking, observing, and understanding — not acting
   B. Predicting and alerting the patient to patterns of sabotage
   C. Setting the stage for interpreting deviations from the frame of treatment in terms of the transference and for marking them as meaningful
   D. Seeing the contract as a transitional object
   E. Making use of the therapist as an object for identification
IV. Self-monitoring by the therapist
   A. Safeguarding the therapist's ability to self-monitor
   B. Marking therapist deviations, or inclinations to deviate from the contract, as meaningful
V. Lowering the likelihood of patient dropout (see chapter 8)

---

implicit, abdicating any responsibility for her actions: "Of course I can't control myself and I act out by hurting myself . . . that's my illness." Defining and discussing each party's contributions to the treatment underlines the fact that the therapist cannot in any realistic way assume all responsibility for the patient's treatment, let alone for her life, and also communicates to the patient that her efforts are essential to the therapy. In addition, this process enables the therapist to explain that in psychodynamic psychotherapy the patient's self-destructive actions are not seen as the illness, but rather as surface phenomena that stem from underlying, unexplored conflicts and that may serve to distract the patient from experiencing the affects associated with those conflicts. Patients with extensive earlier experiences in therapy often report that in prior treatment they had never engaged in any exploratory work because of the ongoing focus on acting-out behaviors.

PROTECTING THE THERAPY

In dynamic therapy the therapist maintains a neutral position in order to experience and observe the forces at work in the patient's psyche. As Kernberg (1984) stresses: "Technical neutrality means maintaining an equal distance from the forces determining the patient's intrapsychic conflicts, not a lack of warmth or empathy" (p. 103). To remain equidistant from the patient's instinctual needs, superego, acting (in contrast to observing) ego, and external reality, the therapist must not fasten onto the manifest level of the patient's discourse. A freely hovering attention is difficult to maintain under any circumstances, but it becomes a significantly greater challenge in the therapy of borderline patients for a variety of reasons: these patients can be profoundly confused; their confusion often seems ego-syntonic; and the problems they present can carry a sense of urgency and threat to life and limb.

Neutrality is threatened any time a therapist feels compelled to intervene in a patient's life, to give advice, or to make a decision for a patient; it is threatened any time a therapist hesitates to speak up in session for fear of what might ensue. When discussing the treatment contract with a patient, therapists must keep in mind that the ultimate goal of the contract is to protect their ability to observe neutrally and reflect calmly on the data emerging in the therapy sessions. This goal guides the specific content of the contract.

Containing the patient's aggression and seduction

Our understanding of the pathology emphasizes the role of unintegrated self- and other-representations, primitive defense mechanisms,
and unmetabolized aggressive drives in creating borderline patients'
chaotic subjective and interpersonal experience. Their aggression can be
directed toward the self or toward another, and can shift back and forth
between self and other in a way that demonstrates fundamental self/
object confusion. The aggression may also be incompletely differenti-
ated from libidinal drives so that therapists working with borderline
patients may find themselves subjected to a confusing mix of aggressive
challenges and seductive appeals.

A therapist who is preoccupied with worries about a patient's
harming herself or drawing the therapist out of the therapeutic role
experiences a strong pull to attend to the manifest level of the patient's
discourse at the expense of investigating the more unconscious and
symbolic meanings. If borderline patients' tendencies to act out are not
contained, their therapists may feel that they are attempting to do
therapy "with a razor blade at their throat." The contract's emphasis on
strict parameters of treatment and clear definitions of responsibility is a
way of communicating to the patient that therapists have no chance of
successfully attending to their task unless the razor blade is put away.
The clinical impression that a patient's self-destructiveness is the greatest stressor experienced by therapists has been supported in a study on
the stresses of psychotherapeutic work (Hellman, Morrison, & Abramowitz, 1986).

Allowing the therapist to feel safe and maintain neutrality

We have reviewed the central role of the therapist's neutrality in psychodynamic psychotherapy. In anticipation of expected pulls away from
neutrality, the contract must define the practical protection of the patient's life as her own responsibility—with the understanding that she
can make use of the surrounding support system as needed (that is,
family, friends, police department, emergency room, hospital admitting
office). Under these conditions the therapist can more easily maintain the
vantage point of observer of the patient's psychic processes without
getting caught up in the turbulence of her life.

Many therapists have found themselves in situations where a small initial interaction outside the frame of the therapy (for example, phone contact) has led to a spiral of involvement, drawing them further and further from their position of neutrality. As the spiral expands, therapists become less available in their unique role of empathic but uninvolved observers of the patient's intrapsychic conflicts. A well-executed contract does not guarantee that patients will not attempt to draw their therapists into real dilemmas, but it facilitates therapists' efforts to remain neutral—both by heightening their early awareness of any deviation from the agreed-upon boundaries of therapy and by aiding their efforts to regain neutrality should it be temporarily abandoned. The contract also signals to the patient that protecting the therapist is as important to the treatment as protecting the patient; if either is unsafe, the treatment is at risk. In a situation where neutrality is threatened, the therapist can refer to the parameters of the therapy established in the contract and encourage the patient to reflect on what the pressure being put on the treatment frame might mean, especially in terms of the transference.

Allowing the patient's dynamics and affects to unfold

There are specific situations where the therapist may deviate from neutrality to intervene when faced with imminent acting out. For example, a therapist may find it necessary to advise a patient on the verge of dropping out of college to defer that decision until the underlying reasons can be explored. The therapist's responsibility is then to reinstate neutrality as soon as possible and to raise the question of why the patient was acting in a way that drew the therapist out of his role. The contract aids the therapist's efforts to contain the patient's tendency to act out by clearly defining a space within which the patient can fully experience her intense affective states while agreeing to take responsibility to translate these feelings and the concomitant impulses into words rather than actions. The therapy could be seen as a bonzai garden in which each branch of the patient's pathology can be expressed on a scale that is not lacking in detail or intensity but that is contained in an observable space. The point of the contract is not to attempt to banish the intense affects of the patient, but to create a setting where they can be safely expressed, contained, absorbed, reflected on, and integrated.

It is our belief that the safer the frame of the therapy, the more easily the intense, confused, internal dynamics of the patient can and will emerge. Another metaphor for contract-based therapy would be a boxing ring. Although the transference may involve intense and concentrated interaction, it is contained by the ropes around the ring and the agreed-upon rules of conduct. Within the transference, therapists may be experienced as adversaries, while within the frame of the treatment they continue to function more as referees, observing the interaction between the patient and the transference object that the patient makes of them. The precision and clarity of the rules help therapists to reflect on a case without becoming preoccupied with or drawn into the manifest level of their patients' conflicts. The contract is thus a means of operationalizing the concept of the "holding environment" (Winnicott, 1965). While the contract does not in itself constitute the holding environment, it provides an interactional frame that, combined with the therapist's stance of neutrality and empathy, creates the holding environment.

An example of the unfolding of the patient's dynamics within the frame of the treatment is provided by a patient who made repeated suicide attempts throughout a previous therapy in which the therapist was experienced as well-meaning and supportive. The patient then sought treatment with a therapist who emphasized during the contract setting that the nature of the treatment would be invalidated if he became directly involved in her suicide attempts. The patient agreed to these terms. In the first phase of the treatment she experienced intense rage at the therapist, repeatedly accusing him of malpractice and verbally attacking him. However, the patient made no further suicide attempts. One way to understand this is that the rage experienced in the sessions and directed at the therapist was the affect that had motivated the suicide attempts. Although the therapy sessions were by no means easy for the therapist, he and the patient had a better chance of observing and understanding that affect when it was contained in the sessions than when it was out of control outside the treatment setting.

INSTRUCTING THE PATIENT

Defining the patient's role

The need to instruct a patient about a treatment that is being considered is characteristic of any form of therapy since individuals come to treatment (as to any situation in life) with their own agendas—both stated and unconscious. A psychoanalyst instructs a new analysand on the method of free association as well as on more concrete issues, such as the policy concerning payments for missed sessions. The psychodynamic therapist beginning with a borderline patient will, in a similar fashion, discuss the patient's role in that method of treatment in addition to issues of scheduling and payment (see examples in chapter 3).

A technical point the therapist must appreciate is the need to review the borderline patient's understanding of the stated conditions of treatment, since the tendency of these patients to distort external reality through the filter of their psychic reality is stronger than that of neurotic patients. A typical example is the patient who agrees during the contract setting that the therapist's role is to help her understand her conflicts and yet who, a few sessions later, accuses the therapist of malicious indifference and withholding for refusing to tell her if she should leave her boyfriend.

Instructing the patient about the therapy and her role in it has both a practical and a therapeutic aspect. If a patient has had no prior experience in psychodynamic therapy, instruction lets her know how to engage in the treatment and, should she become "unknowing" in later sessions, allows the therapist to examine why she has forgotten what had previously been discussed.

The patient has every right to know what kind of treatment is being offered in order to decide whether to choose that treatment. She may not be interested in a therapy in which changes come from working to increase self-understanding; rather, she may be seeking a treatment that provides counselling and active interventions in problem areas. If so, it is best to clarify that this is not the work of psychodynamic psychotherapy. Then the patient can consider the option of dynamic therapy without misconceptions and, if she chooses, look elsewhere for the kind of help she prefers. Therapists too often feel they have failed if a patient does not pursue treatment with them. The true error in clinical practice would be to try desperately to engage a patient who is not interested in the therapy being proposed.

Yet patients are often ambivalent about the help they seek. They may express interest in a therapy based on understanding internal conflicts, but then ask the therapist for practical advice. Conversely, they may say they are seeking counselling, but communicate in other ways that they would prefer to work on a deeper understanding of their problems. In such cases, the therapist may be tempted to interpret resistance in the patient. It is generally advisable to avoid interpretations during the contract-setting work, however, since the therapist might become engaged in therapy before the treatment parameters have been defined and agreed upon.

This is not to say that contradictions should not be addressed. Whenever the patient agrees verbally to some aspect of the contract but behaviorally contradicts her assertions, or when her history is at odds with her apparent agreement to treatment, this should be pointed out to her as a reason for concern. The technique of confrontation can be used to encourage the patient's own reflection on the contradiction. What should be avoided at this stage is speculation by the interviewer about *why*. For example, an interviewer might confront the contradiction of an ambivalent patient who, even while reporting that three prior supportive-counseling therapies provided no lasting help, asked for modifications that would lead the proposed therapy to resemble that kind of treatment.

Predicting patterns of undermining treatment

Data concerning the reasons that prior treatments might have failed are always relevant to setting up the conditions of a new treatment. If certain characteristic patterns of behavior—missing sessions, not talking in sessions, coming to sessions on drugs, and so on—seem to have led to the defeat of prior treatments, these patterns, along with an examination of how the patient proposes to deal with them differently, need to be discussed if she is to begin a new treatment. The therapist could decide that these past patterns pose such a threat to the work of therapy that continuing treatment might be made contingent on the patient's refraining from these behaviors (see chapter 5 for a detailed discussion of how to address threats to the treatment). An additional benefit in delineating the patient's role in prior treatment impasses is pointing out that there may be an identifiable pattern beneath what the patient experiences as chaos and confusion.

Setting the stage for interpreting deviations

This review of past treatments and of the patient's role in therapy also serves the purpose of suggesting that the patient-therapist interaction and the feelings that arise within the context of the therapy may be relevant to the work of therapy. Some patients begin treatment with the idea that discussion of events and relations outside of sessions is the sole avenue of understanding, and that the relationship with the therapist does not reflect the intensity of their "real" problems—their internal conflicts and external dilemmas. By setting up clear parameters for the treatment, the therapist draws attention to the patient-therapist relationship as a potentially complex field that necessitates clearly defined roles and continued observation. By emphasizing these roles and their boundaries, the therapist encourages the patient to reflect on any future deviation from them as a potential source of understanding.

The contract as transitional object

To the extent that the patient does begin to reflect on her relationship with the therapist, the treatment contract may function as a transitional object. Jean Laplanche and J.-B. Pontalis (1973) describe the transitional object as "half-way between the subjective and the objective" (p. 464). The treatment contract defines a very particular interpersonal interaction, an interaction the patient will inevitably distort according to her internal needs, wishes, desires, envies and interdictions, and the filters of her internalized relationship paradigms. The contract sets up reference points with regard to objective reality that the patient may grasp on the conscious level, but that she will only accept fully as her defenses are analyzed.

In this sense, the contract presents as a paradox; it seems to ask the patient to agree to parameters in a relationship and to conditions of treatment that she cannot be expected to maintain given the chaotic and distorted state of her subjective experience. What keeps this from being an impossible position for the patient is the distinction stressed between inner experience and external reality and the therapist's continued references back to the contract as the work of therapy proceeds (Sterba, 1934). (See chapter 7 for a case illustration that focuses on this aspect of the therapeutic process.) While the contract gives the patient free rein in her experience of and fantasies about the therapist, it also directs her to channel these into words and to keep her overt behaviors within clear boundaries. In fact, the latter makes the former possible.

The therapist as an object for identification

Related to the concept of transitional object is that of identification. By focusing on the fact that patient and therapist alike have rights and responsibilities within the frame of the therapy, therapists implicitly offer themselves to their patients as models for identification: they are interested in their own right to safety, the protection of their capacity to think clearly, and the preservation of a space for curiosity and reflection.

THE CONTRACT AND THERAPIST SELF-MONITORING

It is important to remember that it is not only the patients who are at risk of deviating from the conditions of treatment defined by the contract. Therapists are also subject to strong forces that work on different levels of awareness. The pull they experience to make an exception to a contract could seem to come from a very practical, manifest-level issue. It might, for example, seem logical to reduce an agreed-upon fee because a patient's father has cut off her financial support. Before taking any such action, however, therapists would do well to pause; they are about to change a parameter of the treatment. What might be at work beneath the surface? Why are they considering doing this without examining the situation more thoroughly? Is it clear what the patient's role was in her father's action? What else might the patient do in this situation besides ask the therapist for help? What is the meaning of asking the therapist for help? What is being activated in the countertransference that is reflected in the therapist's impulse to take action before thorough exploration? Is the therapist caught up in a process of projective identification (that is, experiencing anger toward the father that the patient cannot tolerate experiencing herself)?

Of course, any therapist would ideally pause at a moment like this to reflect further on the situation. By maintaining a clear belief in the contract as a set of firm arrangements that should never be changed without examining the urge to make the change, therapists may find it easier to return to their task when they are at greatest risk of abandoning the role of neutral observer.

The pull that a therapist experiences to deviate from the established parameters can arise from any number of factors: fear of the patient's anger, fear that the treatment may harm the patient, anger within the countertransference that has been catalyzed by a projective process, and so on. Whatever the case, this urge is a signal to the therapist to reflect on the process of the therapy, as well as on the adequacy of the contract, which may need modification or augmentation.

Summary of Functions of the Contract

Psychodynamic psychotherapy is an arena in which a patient's internalized and largely unconscious object relation paradigms unfold and become available to experience, interpretation, and understanding. The careful framing of the therapy within the confines of the established session times serves to provide a restricted and safe domain within which the patient's dynamics—however threatening, disturbing, or chaotic—can unfold. Ideally, if the treatment alliance is formed and the patient effects a transfer of internalized object relations onto the therapeutic relation, then the maladaptive drive derivatives will be brought into focus in the therapeutic arena, a space reserved for verbal interaction and reflective observation. If the contract succeeds in replacing ambiguity about the nature of the treatment with relative clarity and in promoting the patient's participation and understanding of the process of therapy, then a therapeutic alliance is more likely to emerge. This alliance is an especially difficult balance to achieve in the case of borderline patients since a strong negative transference often threatens it from the start (even if that aspect of the transference has not yet been expressed in explicit terms). Ideally, the discussion of the contract will make it clear to the patient that therapy is strong enough to contain all her feelings—even the most negative ones. This understanding will enhance the development of a true therapeutic alliance, no matter how stormy the treatment may appear on the surface.

Clear, careful, and repetitive work by the therapist is required both to set up these conditions and to maintain them as the therapy proceeds. The frame of treatment is likely to be the target of the patient's urges to act out feelings in ways designed to discharge their intensity. The contract designates acting out as external to the therapy and attempts to establish conditions in which the primitive defense mechanisms of splitting and projective identification can be contained and observed as the patient employs them as an alternative to acting out. In most cases, borderline patients will attempt to involve the therapist beyond the limits of the sessions. Such involvement, while it may appear to be supportive in the short term, could be detrimental to the work of exploratory therapy by leading to: 1) a dilution and confusion of the dynamics present in the session, with a consequent decrease in the possibility of observing and interpreting them; 2) a spreading of the maladaptive behaviors beyond the arena of the sessions; 3) the potential exhaustion of the therapist's patience and ability to be fully available within the therapeutic alliance; and/or 4) a devaluation of the therapy and the therapist.

Our discussion should have made it clear that the contract does more than establish rules about scheduling, payment of fees, and reporting freely what comes to mind. It is a frame, a structure to which the patient can react in any number of ways. While it may be fixed, or even appear rigid, the contract is not meant to suppress the intense intrapsychic life of the patient, but, rather, to allow the intensity to emerge safely. It is important to remember that while the contract defines the frame, the frame is *not* the picture. Rather, the frame allows the picture to develop.

In examining the ways the patient reacts to the frame and to the other person within it, the therapist begins to see into her inner world. Complicating this process is the fact that the therapist is both the other party in the "boxing ring" (the transference object) and the therapist-observer or, to extend the metaphor, the referee. Given the complexity of this role, the therapist's efforts to remain an observer and understand the patient can be enhanced by an internalized attitude of constant self-monitoring with regard to the parameters of the treatment that have been set up with each patient.

Other Models of Treatment

Having described at length the treatment contract in psychodynamic therapy, we will move on to situate this model of the contract both in the broader context of the literature on treatment contracts in general and in relation to two other specific models. In our comparisons, it will be helpful to distinguish between the process and the content of the contract. For example, when we compare our own model with those described in two other therapy manuals, it will be clear that the content of the contract varies with the specific diagnostic group of patients being treated. The process, however, seems to be guided more by the theoretical orientation toward the nature of the patient's resistance.

In this overview of the concept of the contract, we should also address the relationship between the treatment contract and the therapeutic alliance and their differences. We see the treatment contract as a means of facilitating a treatment alliance. The Menninger research group (Frieswyk, Colson, & Allen, 1984) has seen collaboration as the essence of the treatment alliance. In one sense, the main goal of the treatment is to create a genuine collaboration. In contrast, the treatment contract is simply a specification of what is needed to do therapy. The contract lays out the basics without which the work cannot proceed. Therapy with borderline patients involves a paradoxical-appearing therapeutic alliance: the freer the patient feels to express her intensely negative feelings about the therapist and the therapy—within the context established by the contract—the better the alliance.

Review of the Contract Literature

In reviewing the research on the therapeutic contract, David Orlinsky and Kenneth Howard (1986) have isolated key concepts, including the provisions of the contract regarding the concrete parameters of therapy (that is, schedule, term, and fee payment) and the implementation of the contract in promoting the methods of therapy (timeliness, role preparation, conversational behavior, and styles of implementation).

Most relevant to the present discussion are the overall results of numerous studies on formal role preparation for patients prior to the initiation of treatment. These studies show that early role preparation procedures contribute to significantly better outcomes for patients, and, in particular, help those who generally have a poor prognosis (for example, those of a lower socioeconomic status) to benefit from psychotherapy (Frank & Gunderson, 1990; Gunderson, Frank, et al., 1984).

There are also studies on the styles of role implementation, that is, process outcome studies that examine the manner in which therapists and patients implement their contractual roles. A consistent pattern emerges, indicating that a patient's active role collaboration, as opposed to dependency, favors good outcome.

CONTINGENCY CONTRACTING

Donald Meichenbaum and Dennis Turk (1987) have summarized the research on the use of various procedures to enhance patient treatment adherence. They emphasize such procedures as patient education, behavior modification approaches, and teaching self-regulatory skills. Most relevant here is their review of the literature on behavioral contracting, that is, generating a contract that specifies the obligations of each party and the ensuing consequences if the obligations are not met. The contingency contract actively involves the patient; an explicit agreement specifies the expectations, plans, responsibilities, and consequences of the behaviors targeted for change. It may appear ironic that such a contract would be relevent to psychodynamic psychotherapy; on the surface, contingency contracting has little to do with the exploration of unconscious affects, drives, conflicts, and relationship paradigms. However, a point we will return to again and again is that the exploratory work of psychodynamic therapy requires that certain conditions be present in the treatment; the contract describes those conditions. Contract setting has a behavioral element insofar as it specifies that a certain reinforcement—the therapy, to the degree that it is a reinforcement—is not available, is not *possible*, if certain conditions are not met. In addition, one could argue that the "behavioral," aspect of the contract is related to certain psychodynamic notions of the development of the psyche in that the clear, consistent, and predictable structure established by the contract may present the patient with a reliable container for her feelings for the first time in her life—a container that may then be internalized as part of the treatment process.

29

Research (reviewed in Meichenbaum & Turk, 1987) has been done to determine whether behavioral contracts should be written or verbal, negotiated or by fiat, individual or standardized, public or private, and contingent upon outcome or on process measures that affect the contract. From this body of research data, the following guidelines for developing the behavioral contract have emerged. (Keep in mind that these guidelines apply to contingency contracting in general; we are not defining the specific psychodynamic model of the contract we recommend for expressive therapy with borderline patients.)

1. A clear and detailed description of the required instrumental behavior is preferred.
2. Some criteria should be set for the time or frequency limitations constituting the goal of the contract.
3. The contract should specify positive reinforcements contingent upon fulfillment of the criteria.
4. Provisions should be made for some aversive consequences contingent upon nonfulfillment of the contract within a specified time or with a specified frequency.
5. A bonus clause should indicate the additional positive reinforcements obtainable if the person exceeds the minimal demands of the contract.
6. The contract should specify the means by which the patient's response is observed, measured, and recorded; a procedure is stated for informing the patients of their achievements over the duration of the contract.
7. The timing for delivery of reinforcement contingencies should follow the response as quickly as possible.

These guidelines do not take into account either the type of intrapsychic change that is the goal of psychodynamic therapy or the complexities of the therapeutic alliance with borderline patients. Nevertheless, it is interesting and instructive to examine these elements of contingency contracting in order to contrast this model with contract setting in the dynamic treatment of the borderline patient. Although guidelines 3 and 4, positive and aversive reinforcers, are not included explicitly in the dynamic treatment contract, they are involved implicitly. For example, because contact with the therapist is often perceived by the borderline patient as desirable, and even needed, the patient may adhere to the therapy guidelines in order to secure continuation of the treatment.

While psychoanalytic writing has generally avoided the concepts of reward and punishment, Freud ([1912] 1958) quite explicitly stated that what fueled the patient's wish to change was not the ailment or its cost but rather the patient's positive transference and, by implication, the fear of losing the therapist's affection. The therapist is not, however, setting the stipulations as a reward, but rather making it explicit that if certain conditions are not present (for example, showing up on time for sessions, speaking freely without censoring, and taking responsibility for actions), the therapy by its very nature cannot be carried out.

The concepts of contingencies and reinforcements are also relevant to the dynamic treatment contract in that the therapist must rule out the possibility that the patient may attempt to control the therapy and the therapist via suicidal or self-destructive threats and behavior. The therapist must frame the treatment in a way that clearly avoids any reinforcement of acting-out behavior by unintended rewards. For example, a patient with chronic suicidal urges is assigned the responsibility for dealing with such impulses between sessions. This avoids the possibility that she might use these urges to engage the therapist in increasing amounts of contact. Thus, the therapeutic frame does not have a built-in reward for suicidal ideation.

Avoiding unwitting reinforcement of such behavior is not, however, the final goal of this arrangement. This frame is constructed primarily to provide therapist and patient with a sufficiently secure setting in which the motivations behind the patient's impulses and behavior can be examined without forcing the therapist to become so involved around acting out as to preclude objective observation and thoughtful reflection.

Before comparing the contract in the dynamic therapy of borderline patients with the contract in other specific treatment models, we wish to comment on the relevance and inadequacy of some of the fundamental principles and clinical findings we have reviewed here regarding treatment contracts in general as they apply to contract setting with borderline patients. The educational function of the contract is relevant insofar as some borderline patients (whether with or without previous exposure to therapy) may not know what to expect from dynamic psychotherapy.

Probably more relevant to our specific population, however, is the role of the contract in informing the patient of the boundaries of the treatment, thus addressing her characteristic proneness to discharge feelings through action rather than to experience them, express them, and reflect on them. The contract defines the therapy as a space for verbal expression, not action. In addition, the borderline patient, unstable in her identity and often feeling empty, is likely to experience tremendous need for immediate human contact and gratification. Her expectations of therapy are often primitive, magical, and unrealistic. The contract, worked out before the treatment begins, attempts to counter these overwhelming needs and expectations with a message (that will need to be repeated again and again) concerning the real limitations—and potential rewards—of the therapy.

Another general principle of contracts that is borne out in our clinical research is the consistent finding that active patient collaboration is associated with good outcome. Many borderline patients are angry and suspicious, and the early phases of treatment are often not collaborative. We have found in a follow-up telephone interview that many of our patients who dropped out of treatment did so with no warning; they did not tell the therapist they would not be coming to the next session. This uncommunicative, and unilateral, way of ending treatment suggests these patients held back from expressing anger, resentments, objections, suspicions, accusations, or other negative feelings about the treatment. The contracting process, and in particular its exploration of the patient's response to the conditions of treatment, is an effort to elicit resistance and negative transference and to include them in the therapeutic dialogue so that they will not remain underground until acted upon.

Finally, with regard to the relation of contingency contracting to contract setting with borderline patients, the therapist describes to the patient the conditions that are needed to allow the treatment to take place. A simple example of one of these conditions is the patient's regular attendance; a therapist may explain to a patient with a history of sporadic attendance in prior therapies that treatment requires her to attend the sessions and that if she does not show up, she will be making it impossible to continue the therapy. Patients often distort this explanation by seeing the therapist's ending of the treatment as a "punishment" for nonattendance. But, in fact, ending is not the contingency for nonattendance; nonattendance is the ending of the therapy. Therefore, the principle of contingency contracting relevant to the contract setting consists of the therapist pointing out to the patient the contingencies of which she is in control.

The Contract
in Other Treatment Manuals

This is the era of "manualized therapies," termed by some (Luborsky, 1984) a revolution in the teaching and practice of therapy. Researchers doing empirical work in therapy outcome studies saw manuals as an advance in defining specific therapies for purposes of experimentation and replication. For the sake of comparison and contrast, we will describe the contract-setting phase of treatment from our own and two other published treatment manuals. First, Interpersonal Therapy (IPT), a brief treatment that focuses on depressed patients and uses an interpersonal model. Comparing this manual to ours will provide an idea of the difference between working with patients organized at a neurotic level and those with borderline personality organization. We will also compare our process with that of Marsha Linehan, who uses dialectic behavioral therapy (DBT), a cognitive-behavioral approach, with borderline patients. This comparison will elucidate the particular approach needed for dealing with borderline patients as a result of differences both in the conceptualization of the illness and in the treatment strategies and techniques employed.

If we briefly review our own manual for psychodynamic therapy with borderline patients (Kernberg, 1989), we find that it advocates contract setting within the first four to eight sessions, after the diagnostic phase in which the therapist has gathered history and made a formulation. Without an adequate diagnostic impression, the contract setting would be meaningless since the conditions of the contract are rooted in the nature of the pathology, which guides the treatment recommendations.

The contract setting may take several sessions in which the focus is not only on the content of the contract, but also on the process of discussing it. The nature of the contract is spelled out by the therapist and explored by both parties. There are two parts to the contract: the general conditions of therapy, which apply to all patients, and the part that is specific to the individual patient based on her individual history and pattern of treatment impasses.

THE IPT APPROACH

The primary treatment goal in IPT (Klerman et al., 1984) is the alteration of an interpersonal event that underlies the symptom of depression. Starting from a psychodynamic point of view, the symptom is viewed as an expression of interpersonal loss or conflict, including unrealistic and unmet expectations and grief. It follows from this that it is the nature of the patient's interpersonal conflicts that serves as the therapeutic focus rather than the symptom of depression per se. Any change in affect is seen as an indicator that interpersonal difficulties are being resolved, either spontaneously or as a product of the therapy. IPT's focus can vary from addressing behavior change in the patient to increasing her awareness of unconscious processes. Mediating goals of the process include the development of knowledge about the nature of depression and the development of new interpersonal skills.

In the service of these objectives, the therapist provides support through reflection, questions the patient about history and feelings, provides information, and gives direct advice. This array of procedures extends from evocative to directive and from within sessions to between sessions. Homework assignments are included in the treatment, and skills for reducing interpersonal conflict are taught.

In the IPT manual, the therapist is directed to set the treatment contract in the initial sessions. The patient and therapist set treatment goals together, the therapist sometimes helping the patient choose goals that are realistic. In addition, practical aspects of treatment are determined, including length and frequency of sessions, appointment times, and fees. Next, the roles of patient and therapist are defined. The patient's task is to talk about concerns and to discuss material related to the treatment goals.

IPT compared to our treatment

The IPT approach seems straightforward; it assumes that the patient will accept the rationale of the treatment contract. There is no anticipation of resistance or opposition from the patient. It is here that the basic difference between depressed patients (who are assumed to be without Axis-II pathology) and borderline patients (who are sometimes depressed) is most obvious. With their relatively high dropout rate, it must be assumed that the borderline patients' resistance to treatment, combined with their inherent instability, makes it especially difficult for them to benefit from treatment. Addressing their instability, and eliciting and discussing the patients' resistances during the contract-setting phase are what makes the process different from the analogous one used with depressed outpatients. It is interesting, in this regard, that Axis-II patients did not respond as well to IPT in the NIMH multicenter study (Shea et al., 1990).

THE COGNITIVE-BEHAVIORAL APPROACH

Linehan (in press) has described a dialectical behavior therapy (DBT) treatment for parasuicidal women. The term "parasuicidal" refers to behavior that is self-destructive but not lethal. The DBT manual specifies that in the first two sessions of therapy the client is oriented to DBT and given a role-induction interview to provide her with information about her role as client and the therapist's role. This orientation information includes: 1) the theory of parasuicide; 2) the philosophy of the treatment; 3) the rules, limits, and expectations that apply to the client; 4) what the client can expect from the therapist; 5) an outline of the course of treatment with termination dates; 6) the probable response of the therapist to suicidal behavior on the part of the client; 7) the policy regarding confidentiality; and 8) handouts and bibliographic material.

Rules, limits, and expectations of the client

Therapist and client discuss attendance, commitment to reducing self-destructive behavior, and involvement in productive living. Attendance at both individual and group sessions is expected; the client cannot be in individual therapy without being in group, and vice versa. If a group session is missed, the client is expected to view the session on videotape. Missing four sessions in a row will result in termination of therapy.

The client is asked to agree to the specific goal of reducing suicidal behavior. The therapist is attentive to the client's ambivalence regarding the suicidal behavior, and although an explicit verbal commitment to reducing it is the goal, less explicit commitments can be accepted. Finally, the prerequisite for being in DBT is involvement in a productive living situation, that is, engaging in some productive activity on a daily basis. If the client for any reason ends her productive living situation, she has two weeks in which to get into another situation before having her treatment terminated. The client is given the phone numbers of the therapist and the crisis clinic, and is told she can call at any appropriate time.

What the client can expect from the therapist

The therapist will make every effort to conduct DBT as competently as possible. A therapist cannot save the client, cannot solve her problems, and cannot keep her from engaging in suicidal behavior. All the client can expect is the therapist's effort to be supportive, to help her gain insight, learn new skills, and acquire the tools to deal more effectively with her current living situation. It may be useful for the therapist to review misconceptions about therapy, including the notion that the therapist can somehow make everything better.

Probable responses of the therapist to suicidal behavior

The client is informed that the therapist expects a continuation of suicidal behavior since such behavior is a habitual, though maladaptive, response to stress, and habits are difficult to stop. The therapist will make every effort not to reinforce such behavior by giving it undue attention or by overreacting to it. If, however, the client engages in behavior that leads the therapist to think she is at substantial medical risk, the therapist might insist upon hospitalization or other unwanted interventions. The point of view to be communicated is one that respects the welfare of both the client and therapist. Therapists have a right to protect themselves from legal action, from undue anxiety, and from the stress of a client remaining in a setting that requires too much effort on their part to ensure the client's safety.

DBT compared with our treatment

Given the same patient population, it is instructive to compare the cognitive-behavioral strategies and techniques to those of psychodynamic treatment. There are many similarities in approach. Both treatments put an emphasis on the early contract-setting phase of the treatment process with attention to detail. Both emphasize what the therapist will and will not do in the likely event of suicidal behavior on the part of the patient. Both strive for clarity and the establishment of conditions of treatment that will protect the treatment from the maladaptive behaviors of the patient.

The treatments differ, however, in what is considered the most helpful stance of the therapist (active intervention versus neutrality), in what is the essence of the treatment (teaching and learning of skills versus exploration of the patient's unconscious via analysis of the transference), and in expected patient behavior (continued maladaptive behavior until more successful coping skills are learned versus a decrease in self-destructive acting out and a turning of aggression toward the treatment in the form of resistance).

In the differences between the two approaches to the contract, we have both a paradigm and an example of how the cognitive-behavioral and psychodynamic therapist conceptualizes and proceeds with the borderline patient. The rationale and philosophy of DBT are given to the patient in some detail, while this is not done in dynamic therapy. The role of the DBT therapist is not defined principally as an effort to explore and understand the feelings and conflicts that underlie the symptomatic manifestations of borderline pathology. DBT includes an emphasis on didactic skills training as well as on exploration of the patient's inner states. Finally, DBT does not see the re-experiencing of fragmented and unintegrated self- and other-representations within the transference as the central mutative experience of the treatment.

The differences between our approach and others lie in the sense of the process. For example, Linehan (1987, in press) outlines the course of treatment, which, in turn, lends itself to standardization and a more directive approach. In contrast, we are only trying to create and protect a climate. We do not know what is going to happen. Also, we have different expectations for the role-induction part of the contract; people may "know" what to do but may be unconsciously organized against doing it. Our emphasis on the irrational, unconscious forces opposing the work of therapy is what most clearly distinguishes a psychodynamic approach from a cognitive-behavioral one; only by focusing on the irrational for a long time can the rational emerge. After setting a containing frame, we encourage the proliferation of the irrational in the transference while maintaining an appeal to the observing ego through references to the contractual agreement. There is a difference in tone, and, by extension, expectation. Role induction, taken literally, assumes one can talk to all aspects of the person. We do not make that assumption, but work in the hope that the healthy side of the patient is adequately present to begin to work within the frame.

Summary

Our treatment is like that of most other manuals in that it begins the intervention by spelling out the roles of patient and therapist. Yet our manual is unique in its attention to the process of the contract setting as paradigmatic interaction between patient and therapist, and in its inclusion of treatment conditions tailored to the patient's individual history (see chapter 5). Our treatment is also unique in its emphasis on explicitly recalling the contract as a frame and reference point throughout the treatment, especially when any deviation is noted. The emphasis on a clear and carefully considered contract is rooted in the characteristics of the patient population. Impulsivity, affective lability, intense and often undifferentiated aggressive and libidinal drives, identity diffusion, and chaotic interpersonal relations and subjective experience all call for a therapy with a strong and custom-tailored frame.

CHAPTER 3

A Model Contract

THIS CHAPTER BEGINS WITH A discussion of the technique of establishing a therapeutic contract for expressive psychotherapy with borderline patients and then looks at a transcript of a contract-setting session. This interview illustrates several of the problems that arise in attempting to set up a contract.

General Remarks

A treatment contract defines the rights and responsibilities of each of the participants in the therapy. Ideally, it details the *least restrictive* set of conditions necessary to ensure an environment in which the psychotherapeutic process can unfold. Since the contract defines the minimum conditions required for therapy to take place, and since the patient's willingness to accept the contract cannot be known until it is presented to her, the contract setting precedes the beginning of treatment.

The issues raised in attempting to establish the contract concern the fundamental question of whether therapy can take place. Since the contractual issues arise out of the limitations of the therapy rather than the therapist's wishes or personality, the patient's challenge to the contract ("How can you expect me to do this? . . . Isn't this problem what I'm coming to you for?") can be answered objectively ("Whether or not either of us feels you can do this [come to sessions, pay the bill, and so on] is not the question; it is simply a matter of what is necessary to allow this therapy to take place").

Treatment contracts have two components: 1) standard responsibilities (of both the patient and therapist) that are intrinsic to the conduct of any expressive psychotherapy; and 2) particular issues that arise from each patient's individual history and pathology.

The most basic aspects of the contract have to do with universal prerequisites for the treatment: for example, attendance at sessions and payment of fees. If the patient does not agree to these conditions, the therapy cannot take place. In the course of the therapy, minor deviations from these prerequisites might be addressed within the treatment by a combination of confrontation, limit setting, and interpretation. However, any *pattern* of deviation would end the treatment (note that it would be the patient's behavior, not the therapist, that would be ending the treatment).

In addition to the universal prerequisites, the contract may have to address an individual patient's specific patterns of action that have undermined previous therapies. Therapists may need to define clear contingencies vis-à-vis a patient's behavior if the continuation of that behavior would prevent them from carrying out the work of exploratory therapy. For example, therapists might explain to any chronically suicidal or parasuicidal patient that her involving them in a suicide attempt would end the treatment since it would take them out of their role as exploratory therapists.

Further aspects of the contract involve describing patient behaviors necessary to the treatment that are also goals within the treatment, such as reporting thoughts and feelings freely without censorship. These parts of the contract require a commitment and effort from the patient before treatment can begin, but they may constitute a primary topic of treatment before being achieved (see chapter 7 for a case illustration). The main question to keep in mind in setting up the contract is: What are the conditions without which treatment cannot take place? It would be grandiose of any therapist to agree to conditions of treatment that would be likely to undermine the treatment.

Contract setting cannot take place until the patient's history has been obtained. The information that is collected should include the patient's description of her life, the impressions of prior therapists and treating institutions, and most important, the patient's interaction with the diagnostician (as we sometimes refer to the therapist in the precontract phase of the treatment).

PATIENT RESPONSIBILITIES

The areas of patient responsibility that should be routinely discussed with every patient include attendance, fees, and conduct during a session. The patient is expected to come to appointments on time and stay for the entire session. Should the patient have trouble coming to a session, it is her responsibility to inform the therapist as early as possible. A therapist might state, for example:

> You will need to come on time and to leave when the time is up. If you know in advance that you will be unable to come to a session, you will let me know as early as possible. Though there may be a variety of issues that could make coming to a session difficult, it is important that you try to come to each scheduled session.

Though the clinician may view these conditions as eminently reasonable, patients frequently see them as too confining and/or as evidence of the diagnostician's suspicions about their motivation for treatment. The patients' objections may be due to a variety of factors, including fear of being controlled and the wish to be saved without any active effort on their part.

Some therapists may be tempted to pass over this discussion of attendance for fear that it seems too obvious. Indeed, patients have been known to make devaluing remarks in response to this expectation ("I'm here, aren't I?"). Yet, to avoid this issue altogether would be to deny part of the dynamics of borderline pathology: the primitive belief that an ideal other can take care of the patient without any input or effort on the patient's part—without her even being there.

Since the contract-setting phase is designed to determine whether treatment can take place at all and, if so, under what conditions, in-depth interpretations should be avoided. The issue at this point is not why the patient objects to the minimal conditions but, since they are essential, if the patient is willing to work within these conditions. Treatment cannot take place without this agreement. The therapist should make a matter-of-fact statement like the following:

> I understand that there are many reasons why this might appear difficult for you. Indeed, I expect that looking at some of these reasons will form an important part of our work together, should we agree to begin treatment. However, at this point what is important to note is that if you are not here, no work can go on. From time to time it may be difficult for you to come to or stay in the sessions, but you will need to discuss those difficulties with me rather than act on them by not appearing.

The issue of fees includes what the fee per session is, how the patient will be billed, when the bill should be paid, and also the policy on missed appointments. There may be a discussion of the fee if the therapist charges on a sliding scale that depends on the patient's means. Different therapists may employ different policies regarding missed sessions, rescheduling, and when payments are due. The essential point with regard to contract setting is not which policy therapists feel comfortable with, but rather that they describe a consistent policy on which they are prepared to follow through. Establishing the ground rules regarding the fee at the outset establishes an anchoring point to which the therapist can return if the situation warrants.

Consider the case of a patient who, once therapy has begun, has failed to pay her bill for two months. At the same time, she has been passionately proclaiming her rage that, given her history of early maternal deprivation, her traumatic past does not exempt her from responsibilities in her adult life: "It's just not fair. Someone should make it up to me. Then I might get over my anger." In such situations, therapists might be tempted to forego any discussion of the errant bill. However, the contract-setting sessions remind them that they have a responsibility to raise the issue with the patient in spite of any reluctance they may experience. Indeed, it may be that the therapists' hesitation corresponds to the affective significance of this material within the transference and that discussing the material would be the best intervention they could make at that moment.

PATIENT ROLE IN METHOD OF TREATMENT

Every type of psychiatric treatment, including somatic therapy, requires some form of patient participation if the treatment is to be carried out correctly. Asking the patient to participate in her own treatment and, more important, telling her that the outcome depends on her active participation allays the patient's fear of dependency, frustrates her wish for dependence, and challenges her sense of entitlement.

Edward Bordin (1979) emphasizes that the three crucial elements of a treatment alliance are an agreement on goals, an assignment of tasks, and the development of bonds. The first two touch on this initial phase of contract setting. Without an agreement on goals, there can be no common purpose. Without the assignment of tasks, there can be no consensus about who is to do which part of the work. Frequently, borderline patients have had several prior therapy experiences, including a variety of different task assignments, some in contradiction to others. It is essential to clarify the nature of each task, including its relevance to this particular form of treatment.

Expressive psychotherapy with borderline patients is based on psychoanalytic principles that are modified only to the extent made necessary by the borderline person's rudimentary ego. Free association is encouraged, except when issues of suicide, homicide, or threats to the treatment emerge, at which point the patient must so inform the therapist. Thus, a statement about saying "whatever comes to mind" is essential because this treatment relies on making connections between conscious and unconscious material, a task requiring uncensored verbalizations. A typical informational statement about the method of treatment might be:

> Your role in therapy is to speak freely about whatever is on your mind, particularly in relation to the main problems that brought you here, with the goal of understanding the unknown motivations for your behavior. Although at times it may feel difficult for you to do this, it is important to speak your mind without censoring it; you can include thoughts, feelings, dreams, fantasies, and so on. Your thoughts may take the form of a question for me. Should that be the case, I may or may not answer, depending on what I feel to be most therapeutic in that instance. Beyond the general rule of speaking freely in session, if

something is happening in your life where you run the risk of harming yourself or others or where the continuity of the treatment might be affected, then your responsibility is to bring that issue up before anything else. For example, if you suddenly found out that you'd be moving out of the area, it would be important to bring that up for discussion before talking about whatever else might come into your mind.

THERAPIST RESPONSIBILITIES

The very fact that therapists enunciate their own responsibilities concretizes their belief that therapy is a two-way street. Responsibility defines involvement, in turn underscoring the work aspect of the treatment. The therapists' principal responsibilities have to do with the scheduling of appointments, attending to the therapy during the sessions, limiting their involvement with their patients to the work of exploratory therapy, and maintaining appropriate confidentiality.

Clinicians inform their patients about the scheduling of appointments, including arrangements of time as well as procedures for notifying patients if they will be away. They should state clearly, succinctly, and without apology, both their intended behavior and what would happen should they have to cancel. For example:

> I will provide you with two regular sessions a week at times we need to work out jointly. The meetings will be forty-five minutes in length and will take place in my office. Unless I have an emergency, I will tell you one month in advance when I am planning not to be in the office. My policy for making up appointments I am unable to keep is . . .*

The statement about fees has important clinical implications. In announcing that they are to be paid, clinicians are declaring that the service provided has a value for which they expect compensation. Though the statement about fees can be made in a few words, much is communicated attitudinally. Clinicians who cough, lower their voice, or look away while stating the fee are making an important statement.

*A specific policy is not described here because any number of therapist polices may be appropriate. Our teaching of the contract is meant to increase awareness of the principles involved and relevant techniques. Clinical judgment can then guide the therapist's choice of specific policies.

Similarly, clinicians who, out of guilt, decide they "must" work with a patient, may announce the fee angrily, as if to suggest, "I'll work with you, *but* you'll pay plenty for me." And therapists who experience doubts about their ability to help a patient may discuss the fee in an apologetic tone, suggesting that they may not be able to provide the patient with "her money's worth."

Ideally, clinicians will discuss fees as they would any other subject. This is especially important given borderline patients' tendency to distort excessively the meaning of the fee to therapists. Therapists should inform each patient that their efforts are being compensated for by the money received from the patient and that they require from the patient nothing more and nothing less for their services. The patient, therefore, can neither reward nor punish a clinician by the progress she makes. The fee is for the clinician's time and effort, not for any particular outcome.

THERAPIST ROLE IN METHOD OF TREATMENT

Diagnosticians need to make several statements about how they will function in the treatment. One of the aims of any treatment contract is to educate the patient about the nature of the particular therapy being considered. It would be naive to assume that even those patients who have been in treatment in the past intuitively know or have come to recognize the responsibilities of each of the participants. Transference in borderline patients is particularly stormy, given their chaotic inner world and difficulty with reality testing. They will frequently distort the nature of the therapeutic process and the clinician's responsibilities therein. Nevertheless, it is also true that, on some level, the patient can hear and remember what is being said.

It is not necessary that clinicians make Herculean efforts to describe what their participation will be. Should they find themselves engaged in repetitive efforts to describe their role, they should wonder with the patient if she may be understanding them but objecting to what they are saying. Again, the nature of the resistance would not be explored at this time, but should there be an agreement to begin the treatment, this would be a potential topic for future examination.

The following statement regarding the therapist's role includes some discussion of the clinician's focus on listening and trying to help the patient gain understanding, the rules that are used to guide the therapist's choice of when to speak, the fact that there will be no physical contact, and the nature of confidentiality:

> My responsibility is to listen as attentively as I can to what you are saying and to make comments when I feel they might be helpful. There may be times when you will ask questions that I may not answer and/or there may be times when you want me to speak and I will feel it is in the best interest of the treatment for me to remain silent. There may well be times when you want me to give advice or tell you what to do or comfort you. This form of therapy aims at your arriving at your own decisions, and therefore my position will be to try to help you to understand what it is that you want, rather than for me to tell you what to do or act for you.
>
> What we say here is a private matter between us. I will give out no information unless we first discuss it here and agree together that it makes sense, and then I will ask you to provide me with a written authorization before releasing the information.

It may be necessary with patients who have a previous history of suicide or violent outbursts to add:

> The only exception to this rule would be if you were to pose a threat to your life or anyone else's, in which case you will force me to take whatever steps are necessary, which may include violating confidentiality, to protect you or whoever else might be involved.

It is important for therapists to feel comfortable with the role they are describing. Novice therapists sometimes fail to appreciate the importance and difficulty their role in exploratory therapy entails. These therapists are likely to take to heart the common criticism that they are "sitting there doing nothing" in the face of the patient's pain and chaos. They may become vulnerable to abandoning their position of neutrality and intervening more "actively" with the patient. This form of devaluing criticism is the counterpart to the patient's primitive belief that an all-powerful other could magically fix them and is not doing so only because of sadistic withholding. In reality, devoting one's concentration to the chaotic unfolding of the patient's inner world is a major undertaking, and the therapist is likely to be the only person in the patient's life who is available to take on that role.

46

Depending on the patient's history and presentation, therapists may want to spell out more explicitly the limits of their involvement with the patient, specifically that the therapeutic endeavor is restricted to verbal interaction within an office setting during the established session times except in cases of true emergencies. For example:

> The therapy will take place during our regularly scheduled sessions and within the time frame we have agreed upon. There may be times when you wish to communicate with me outside the sessions either by phone, by mail, or in person. In most instances, I will indicate to you that the appropriate place for such a discussion is in the office at our regular times. This form of therapy aims at your arriving at your own decisions. That may mean that I will, for example, not return your phone call or answer your letter.

The limits of the therapist's involvement in the treatment may have to be elaborated in more detail if, for example, the patient has a history of intruding on prior therapists' privacy; this specific example will be discussed in chapter 5.

Before turning to that part of the contract that deals with specific threats to the treatment posed by the patient's particular pathology, it is necessary to say a few words about setting the treatment contract as an interactive process. There is far more to the creation of the frame than simply reciting a checklist of mutual responsibilities. Clinicians, often for countertransference reasons, may fail to articulate fully either their or the patient's responsibilities. For example, clinicians who find themselves confronted by a challenging, devaluing patient may choose to postpone mentioning all of the patient's responsibilities, telling themselves the patient needs to be eased into therapy. Whenever clinicians avoid discussing an aspect of the contract, they are indicating some counter-transference issue. If clinicians cannot allow themselves to describe what is required for treatment to take place, then that difficulty in articulation will manifest itself later in treatment in their avoiding interpreting the patient's grandiosity or aggression or entitlement.

In a different version of this problem, clinicians may articulate fully the areas of responsibility but then undo their statements in a variety of ways. For example, diagnosticians who have already discussed and set a fee with the patient might then add, "So we've agreed on a fee of X dollars but if that's too difficult for you, you can pay less." Or, similarly, after having agreed that one of the patient's responsibilities is to come to the session on time, the diagnostician may equivocate, "Of course there will be days when you can't get to a session on time and in those cases I'll try to make up for the lost time at the end of the session." Another possibility is that the words can be letter perfect but the "melody" may present an altogether different picture. Consider those diagnosticians who, obviously very anxious about what they are doing, race through their presentation of the patient's responsibilities, then quickly add, "I don't imagine you have any questions, so I'll just go on."

EVALUATION OF THE PATIENT'S HEARING WHAT WAS SAID

Once clinicians have stated their or the patient's responsibilities, they must carefully observe the patient's response in order to evaluate the significance of these issues to the patient and to begin to observe transference patterns. Is it clear that the patient has heard what the diagnostician has said and, if so, is it clear what her reaction is?

A patient's willingness to listen to the terms of the contract is not an all-or-nothing phenomenon. Blatant denial represents the lowest level. One step above that is the patient who says, "I can't really afford to listen to what you're saying. I just have to be in therapy. I'll do it any way you want."

Next, there is the patient who brushes off what the diagnostician is specifically addressing with a general statement about her commitment to treatment. Unlike the previous patient described, this person is not saying that she must have the treatment, but rather that her commitment should be so obvious that she fails to understand how anyone could question her allegiance or ask her to consider conditions of treatment. Often the matter-of-factness of the patient's assertion distracts the diagnostician from recognizing that the patient has failed to address the specific issue at hand. For example, a patient may respond to the parameter around paying the fee by saying, "You seem to be worried about my paying the bill, but it should be obvious to you that I wouldn't be here if I didn't want to have therapy and wasn't committed to it." The implied accusation here is, "How dare you question my motives and commitment and refer to my history when I am here today giving my all?"

In the most extreme case, where the patient does not take in what the diagnostician is saying, she may close her eyes during the statement, act bored, gaze out the window, or even try to talk over the clinician. If this occurs, clinicians should inform their patient that they have observed her reaction and, in light of this, wonder what the patient has heard. Clinicians should identify the patient's behavior and explain their reason for asking her what she has heard and what it means to her. When patients refuse to acknowledge what clinicians have said or claim that they said something else, diagnosticians should ask the patients what they believe the issue to be. For example, diagnosticians might ask what the patient makes of the fact that though the same statement has now been repeated twice, she continues to insist that she has heard something different. What does she think might be the motivation behind the diagnostician's allegedly saying one thing and yet claiming to have said something else?

If, after confronting the patient with her belief that clinicians would misrepresent their own statements, she cannot resolve that issue, the diagnostician is obligated to declare that they have reached an impasse:

> Either I am lying to you or you are misrepresenting what I have said and cannot allow yourself to review your behavior. In either case there is no basis for our going forward. We can either stop or stick with this if you are interested in reconsidering both possible explanations of the impasse.

Rarely is the situation that extreme. Generally the patient does not completely deny what has been said, but rather indicates that she has heard the words but refuses to think about their implications. The patient may say such things as, "I hear what you're saying about the therapy, but I'm much more comfortable playing it by ear," or may present herself as being so victimized by her pathology or by the therapist that she is "forced" to make an agreement. "I have to say yes. What other choice do I have?" In those instances the clinician needs to point out that the patient does have a choice not to enter into this form of treatment and that the therapist also has a choice, which is to not treat the patient. Diagnosticians should try to frame their position as being reactive to their patients. After the clinician has enunciated the minimal conditions for the treatment, it is the *patient* who says that she cannot or will not adhere to them.

EVALUATION OF THE PATIENT'S ACCEPTING WHAT IS SAID

Further along in the process is the patient who has heard everything that the diagnostician has described but who does not accept all of it and thoughtfully questions it. As with willingness to hear, willingness to accept exists on a continuum. At one end is the patient who rejects the idea of a contract per se. Particularly with narcissistic patients, the very idea of any kind of contract offends their sense of entitlement and results in massive refusal to cooperate. At times the objection is presented in a challenging way: "If I have to say that I agree to these things, then you're not the doctor for me." Or the narcissistic injury may be as great, but the patient more adept at concealing it from the diagnostician: "I think we'd do better without these rules. We could just start meeting and see how we work together."

A slightly less entrenched position is taken by the patient who does not totally reject the idea of rules and a contract, but insists on substituting her own for those the diagnostician proposes. "I can't really accept your rules about paying for missed sessions or saying everything that comes to mind. I think it would be fair if I didn't pay for a session if I really can't get there, and I think you should understand if I don't tell you everything on my mind because some of it is too embarrassing." Or, the patient may superficially agree but signal that she is dismissing any real consideration of the contract by the very facility of her agreement to it. For example, the patient may interrupt the diagnostician before the statement is even completed and say, "Oh yes, I'll give it a shot; I'll try."

Still further along the continuum of accepting the treatment is the patient who does not claim to agree with all aspects but presents no major objections to the basic conditions and shows she has considered them; there is a "yes, but" quality to the agreement. "I understand what you are saying about reporting whatever comes to mind here, but I'm not sure I can do it." The patient who is able to present her objections in a thoughtful fashion is more likely to collaborate with the therapy than someone who initially endorses every aspect without any reservations. In fact, when the latter is the case, the diagnostician should wonder aloud, "How is it that you have no questions or reservations whatsoever to any part of what I have said?"

REACTING TO THE PATIENT'S RESPONSE

One party cannot set a treatment contract. A treatment contract requires an interactive process; it is the outcome of an ongoing dialogue. The diagnostician, having presented the general conditions for the treatment and listened carefully to the patient's reaction, must decide whether to accept the patient's response as adequate for beginning the therapy or to pursue exploration of the patient's implicit or explicit opposition to the contract. The appropriateness of the diagnostician's pursuit of what the patient has said can be viewed on a continuum. The least appropriate response would be an apology, withdrawal, or abdication. For example, in response to a patient's vehement denunciation of the idea of any contract at all, the diagnostician might say, "Well, this may be too much to ask all at once. We can see if we can work towards it." It is important to note that at the moment we are not considering those aspects of the treatment contract that are designed in response to pathology that is specific to a given patient. Rather, the discussion thus far has centered on the minimal requirements for conducting an exploratory psychotherapy. These are conditions of the therapy, not of the therapist, though the patient often responds as if the latter were the case.

Consider the situation where the diagnostician has stated the necessity of coming twice a week and the patient categorically refuses to come more than once a week or to investigate the basis of her objection. Clinicians who then respond, "If you feel that it's too difficult to come to two sessions a week, then we can begin by having only one session per week," are not carrying out the task of establishing what they believe to be the minimum requirements for conducting the treatment. If, on the other hand, the diagnostician feels that the number of sessions is an open question and, in fact, subject to discussion, then a fixed number should not have been presented as a contractual issue in the first place. The clinician could have invited the patient's collaboration by saying, "While I'm recommending expressive therapy to you, it's not clear how many times a week we should meet. What are your thoughts about that?"

A different version of the diagnostician's withdrawing from the conditions of the contract would be to ignore the patient's objections and act as if an agreement to begin the treatment had been reached. Accepting a pseudo-agreement sidesteps confrontation.

A more advanced but still incomplete position is represented by the diagnostician who takes up the contractual dilemma to the extent of asking for further clarification, but still fails to confront the specific issues that threaten the contract. For example, the diagnostician might ask, "Tell me more about why you may not be able to come to sessions regularly?" and, after the patient replies that she may need extra hours for her studies, makes no further comment and moves on to another issue. Closer to the optimum diagnostic intervention is the case of the clinician who several times works appropriately with the patient about her objections but who eventually abandons the issue without indicating what the lack of resolution implies about the status of the agreement. Patience, persistence, and repetition are hallmarks of a therapist's work with a borderline patient. Certainly there will be the patient who, though not fully endorsing what has been recommended, indicates enough willingness to comply that the diagnostician feels that the treatment can begin. In those instances it is important for diagnosticians to indicate their awareness that the issue remains somewhat unresolved and to point out the potential dilemma lurking behind the apparent agreement.

A patient whose history included leaving several relationships when they threatened to become too close appeared shocked when the diagnostician wondered about her ability to attend sessions on a regular basis. She insisted that "one thing had nothing to do with the other" and "I can assure you that I will always come to sessions." The clinician explained the basis for concern and, having established that the patient could appreciate why the issue had been raised, accepted her statement, adding that it would not be surprising if, at some point in the treatment, the patient felt the wish to flee. She was urged to be on the lookout for such feelings and to report them should they arise.

Often a patient's behavior during diagnostic sessions is at odds with her verbal agreement. If so, the diagnostician needs to address the apparent contradiction: "Though you've agreed to come twice a week if we decide to begin treatment, you've already missed two sessions during our diagnostic phase."

Specific Threats to the Treatment

Thus far we have discussed only the general arrangements any patient engaged in exploratory psychotherapy would need to agree to. A major goal of the diagnostic phase is to anticipate which situations the patient is likely to create that could threaten the treatment, and to devise parameters to reduce this threat.

This part of the contract-setting process is the most individualized, subtle, and complex. Consequently, we have devoted chapter 5 to a detailed discussion of the most common types of threat to treatment, as well as ways to develop contract contingencies that address them. In this chapter, our discussion will emphasize the principles that inform clinical thinking about this part of the contract.

In formulating the specific issues that need to be taken up with an individual patient, it is important that the clinician pay particular attention both to what transpired in previous therapies—especially those factors that have resulted in disruptions and/or terminations of the treatment—and to here-and-now interactions with the diagnostician. The patient's attitudes and behaviors with the clinician are especially useful since they do not depend on reports from someone else (patient, previous therapist, family) but are actually observed as they occur between the therapist and the patient.

In theory, this is information that both partners can agree on, though the extent to which this does not happen provides valuable information about the status of any agreement and about the dynamics unfolding in the patient-therapist dyad. For example, if the patient has been late for three of her diagnostic interviews, it would be remiss of the clinician to fail to mention that lateness might be an issue in the treatment and to discuss how they might plan together for that contingency.

Ideally, behaviors that have the potential for threatening the treatment will surface in the diagnostic phase, and presumably patient and diagnostician will agree that these activities have occurred, even though they may differ as to their implications. In our example, although both may agree that the patient has come late for several sessions, the patient may argue that this in no way prognosticates her behavior "once the therapy begins." At the very least the clinician needs to explore the basis for the patient's reassurance and, unless it makes sense, to include it as an issue in the contract.

The data collected during the history-taking phase is used to select the specific issues to address in the contract-setting phase. The patient's prior treatment history is second only to the patient's behavior with the clinician in yielding data about likely threats to the treatment. Not infrequently borderline patients, even at a relatively young age, have an extensive treatment history. It is particularly important to learn what the patient had expected of her treatment(s), treater(s), and herself; how, if at all, her experience resulted in modifying her expectations; what role she felt she played in the demise of any prior treatment; in what way she would have liked the treatment done differently; if she can realistically evaluate these expectations, based on prior treatment contacts; and how she would incorporate that knowledge into the construction of a new treatment setting.

Obviously, it is important to contact the prior therapists and, having received their perception of the situation—and their permission—to share it with the patient, paying particular attention to how the patient deals with any discrepancies between her perception and theirs. The clinician should explain to the patient the reasons for any particular concerns, citing the exact information the patient provided that signalled to the clinician the need for discussion and a plan of intervention. "Since you have told me that three therapies ended because you called the therapists at home every night, we need to discuss a policy on phone calls before we start so we can protect this treatment from what has happened in the past." The clinician then observes the patient's response to this comment to determine how seriously the patient takes her own behaviors.

By focusing on the patient's past or present behavior, the clinician communicates that any decision about what constitutes a threat to the treatment derives directly from the patient's own actions rather than from the therapist's arbitrary or capricious judgment. Therapists are able to deal with a patient's challenge, "Why are you doing this to me?" by explaining that it is the patient who is forcing them to respond in this way rather than the clinicians who are imposing their will on the patient. "Since you have come drunk to the last two sessions and, by your own admission, have not been able to think clearly, it is not that I am insisting that you stop drinking but rather you who are telling me that drinking is interfering with your thinking, and therefore with your sessions. Since you want help with how you think about yourself, you are telling me that you cannot drink *and* come to sessions."

In assessing what might constitute a threat to the therapy, it is important to remember that the fundamental task of the contract is to establish a frame within which the treatment process can unfold, to create and preserve an environment where clinician and patient are sufficiently protected that each can carry on his or her respective tasks. The patient must be able to do her best to keep herself and the clinician apprised of all that is going on within her, as well as be open to the impact of the therapist and the therapeutic process on her beliefs, feelings, and reactions. In order to comment therapeutically, therapists must be able to listen as openly as possible, to make use freely of their own knowledge, past experience, and experience of the therapy, and also be willing to change their minds as material evolves. Nothing within the treatment process should threaten either the patient or the diagnostician to the extent that he or she is no longer able to participate in a spontaneous and imaginative fashion.

Potential threats to the treatment may include: 1) poor attendance or inadequate participation in the sessions; 2) problems created outside the sessions that obstruct the conduct of the therapy; and 3) self-destructive or homicidal impulses or actions. Examples of the first type are missing sessions, coming to sessions in a drugged state, and failing to maintain sufficient income to pay for therapy. External problems that threaten the treatment might include a patient's colluding with a family member's prohibiting her from attending sessions, arranging to have a family member threaten to sue a diagnostician who fails to cure the patient, alienating a family member whose financial support is necessary for the treatment, and so on. Problems of the third type—a patient's threats to harm herself or the therapist—can create such tension that they prevent the therapist from thinking freely and spontaneously within the session.

Though in principle the procedure for setting up a treatment contract around specific threats is the same as that already discussed regarding contractual principles relevant for all patients, there are some differences. Patients are generally more accepting of the "generic" treatment rules than of those that address their own actions or attitudes. They may claim that their past behavior has been exaggerated, misrepresented, or is no longer valid. Therefore, the first order of business for diagnosticians is to articulate what they see as the particular threat to the treatment and to ask their patient whether she can empathize with their concern.

The issue here is not the patient's agreement with the clinicians' judgment but only, given the facts, whether she can appreciate that the diagnosticians think this way. If their patient can empathize with the diagnosticians' concern, then they would proceed to examine what steps might be taken to ensure the safety of the treatment. If, however, their patient cannot appreciate their concern, they should then present the evidence upon which they have based their conclusion. For example, they might say,

> Two of your previous therapists said that the reason treatment ended was because you came drunk to several sessions, and I observed you to have slurred speech in our last meeting. That is why I am concerned about your coming to sessions drunk and why I feel we have to think about ways to prevent this from happening.

Should their patient fail to acknowledge the validity of the concern after the data have been presented, then diagnosticians have no recourse but to declare that a treatment contract is not possible. In those instances it is preferable that diagnosticians frame their comment in such a way as to keep open the possibility that their patient might at a later date seek out therapy when she is more willing to consider the relevance of the diagnosticians' comments. For example, the patient might be told,

> It is clear at this point that you and I cannot agree that your drinking poses a threat to the treatment. From your perspective, I am exaggerating the facts. However, my own experience with you, as well as the experience of others which has been reported to me, makes it clear to me that any treatment effort begun with this much risk is not only likely to fail but would also put me in a position of supporting what I view as an unrealistic assumption of yours—that you can continue to drink heavily and, at the same time, fully participate in your treatment. I do not know why you insist on maintaining this belief and, indeed, if you were to begin treatment, that would be an issue that would be very important to investigate. At this point, however, you

leave me no choice. Effective treatment cannot be carried out under these conditions.

In the case of the patient who appreciates that the diagnostician might be concerned, the latter's next step is to invite the patient to participate in a plan to safeguard the treatment against the threat. "How might we protect the treatment against the danger of your suicide threats, a danger that has resulted thus far in the destruction of three treatment efforts and your nearly losing your life?" In the course of the discussion the diagnostician carefully evaluates the patient's attitude toward this collaboration. Does the patient seem to mock the efforts? Does she appear to be "going along" but without conviction? Does what the patient suggests show she is taking seriously the threat and does what she offers seem to have a reasonable chance of success? How amenable is the patient to the diagnostician's suggestions? Is the patient flexible both in her own suggestions and in her reception of the diagnostician's, or does she rigidly maintain her position at all costs? The most reassuring evidence of the patient's cooperation would be her active participation in the construction of the plan while, at the same time, cognitively and affectively voicing her concerns and objections.

The Limits of Contract Setting

The contract spells out those issues that appear to pose a threat to the treatment process and proposes a plan to prevent the treatment from being destroyed. It would be naive to assume that establishing a contract requires that all resistance be abolished before the treatment can begin. Somewhere between the blanket refusal to do anything, that is, "But doctor, if I could do that already, I wouldn't need to be here," and total eradication of the problem is the point at which the contract phase is over and the treatment begins. For example, in the case of a patient whose anorexia had brought her to near-starvation levels on two previous occasions, a contract was established in which the patient agreed to have her weight monitored by a nurse practitioner and, if it fell below a certain level (which was still far from life threatening), to take sustenance supplements. The aim of this arrangement was to preserve the continuity of the exploratory therapy by referring practical management of the patient's weight outside the therapy while recognizing that, for the present, her anorexic urges would remain a problem.

The majority of patients will agree to a contract, although some patients make clear during the contract-setting phase that they are opposed either to acknowledging the ways in which they may threaten the feasibility of treatment or to doing anything to reduce the power of that threat. In such instances, treatment should not be undertaken. For example, a patient whose history is replete with failures to pay her bill and who does not recognize the threat that such behavior would predictably pose to the current treatment, or who recognizes that such a threat would exist but sees it as only the diagnostician's problem, is not in a position to begin the treatment.

Setting the contract defines the limits of responsibility of each of the participants. Clinicians, who may find themselves caught up in the turbulent eddies of countertransference, can use the contract to monitor whether their actions are motivated by their own needs or the patient's. For example, if, in the course of treatment, patients bombard their therapists with accusations of coldness and insensitivity, arousing countertransference suspicions that the patients' condemnations are accurate, the clinicians may have a hard time assessing whether refusing to answer their patients' phone calls is proof of the validity of the accusation. If a patient has a prior history of incessant calling to previous therapists, however, and the issue has been discussed as a potential threat to the current treatment, the therapist, at the moment of doubt as to the motivation, can reflect on the prior agreement and recognize that the thought that he or she may be harming the patient by refusing to answer the phone calls runs counter to the agreement, and therefore signals a countertransference issue. This awareness helps therapists to avoid acting out by accepting the calls.

Setting the contract also has the following additional benefit for the therapy. Should the patient begin to deviate from the agreement at any point in the treatment, the clinician can refer to the contract and question what aspect of the current situation might be responsible for the change:

> Before the treatment began we agreed that your urge to sabotage your therapy might surface in the form of your dropping out of school, resulting in your father's no longer paying the bill. Now you tell me

you're not studying and are thinking of not taking your exams. What's going on here that's causing you to put the treatment in jeopardy?

As in the first section of this chapter regarding general responsibilities within the treatment, the issue of threats to the treatment also calls on diagnosticians' efforts to include both an adequate articulation of the nature of the problem and sensitive and judicious responsiveness to the patient's reactions. Contract setting does not eradicate the problem; it does alert both patient and diagnostician to the nature of the threat as well as to the necessity to construct a plan to contain the danger. Also, it provides the clinician with a reference point to return to should the threat emerge in the ensuing treatment: "As we discussed before beginning our work together, your tendency to X has surfaced. We will need to find out why this is occurring at this time, but first we must make certain that the part of you that wishes to end the treatment does not succeed."

The Contract-Setting Interview

We will now examine a contract-setting interview, paying particular attention to those segments that indicate the patient's resistance to the process as well as to how those resistances were handled.

> THERAPIST: Today we'll be meeting to set up a contract, to see what responsibilities we would each have and what we would need to do in order to be able to work together, *(pause)* unless, of course, anything has come up since last time *(referring to the previous history-taking session)* that you think is so important that we can't go on to this step.
>
> PATIENT: We can go on.
>
> THERAPIST: Okay. Your first responsibility would be to come to sessions. As we talked about, the sessions will be twice a week for forty-five minutes. If for any reason you are unable to come to a session and know about it in advance, your responsibility would be to bring that up for discussion.
>
> PATIENT: But what if I don't know it in advance?
>
> THERAPIST: For example?

PATIENT: If half an hour before a session my car breaks down or
. . . or whatever form of transportation I was counting on doesn't
work, what do I do then?

THERAPIST: I would think you would do two things. You would try
your best to find an alternative method of transportation to
come here, and if that was not possible, you would call me. In
the next meeting we might discuss how this came about and
what it meant to you. *(Pause. Interviewer waits to see if patient
wishes to comment.)*

A second responsibility is paying the fee. As we discussed
in our first meeting, my fee is $95.00. I will give you a bill at the
end of each month and expect you pay to it by the 15th of the
following month.

In terms of what issues to address, I would expect that you
would first present whatever was of immediate urgency to you
and if there was nothing urgent then you would say whatever
comes to your mind without censoring your thoughts or
feelings.

PATIENT: Mmm. I don't know . . . I mean there are certain things
that you just don't talk about, that you just . . . that are hard to
talk about, that I might not want to bring up.

THERAPIST: You're mentioning several issues: things that you don't
talk about, that you don't want to talk about, and that are
difficult to bring up. In terms of things that you don't talk about,
in this treatment, by definition, there is no issue that is off limits.
Of course, some issues may be harder than others to talk about.
Those topics are especially important to identify. I can imagine
you saying for example, "I find topic X very hard to talk about,"
and then discussing what you think makes it hard for you.

Comment

Acknowledging that the patient will find some areas particularly difficult, the interviewer informs her that although the purpose of the
treatment is not to create discomfort, her discomfort does signal an issue
of psychological importance that they should examine. The interviewer,
acting as information-provider, fulfills a task essential to beginning a

treatment by giving the patient a concrete example of how the therapy would proceed if she found herself struggling with a difficult subject ("I can imagine you saying for example . . ."). Note that what the interviewer is describing is that the analysis of the resistance takes precedence over any other content.

PATIENT: But what if I can't? What if I just can't? What if it's something . . . I mean I can see talking about things that happened during the day or what happened yesterday, but there are certain areas of a person's life that shouldn't . . . not really shouldn't, that might be better left not talked about.

THERAPIST: As I mentioned before, it's not always clear what is and is not important and what connections there might be between things that are consciously troubling you and other events in your life. It might be, for example, that you tell yourself something shouldn't be talked about because the subject is one you're afraid to examine.

Comment

Again the interviewer indicates that he understands that there will be issues the patient will find difficult and that the psychotherapeutic approach to events differs from how one thinks about life outside of a therapeutic situation: difficult topics will be examined rather than avoided; customary ways of identifying what is and is not relevant will not necessarily apply.

The interviewer again provides a concrete example of what the patient might anticipate once the therapy begins and, by doing so, sets the stage for later interpretive work should the patient feel the interviewer is criticizing her. Later on in the treatment, for example, the therapist might build on the contract by saying: "You now have the feeling that talking about your family is not the right thing to do because it constitutes a betrayal of them. I mentioned before we started that you might find yourself feeling that there are subjects that shouldn't be talked about as a way of protecting yourself from finding out things that might be threatening to you. Here we have the first such instance."

> Patient: *(Long pause)* Go on *(clearing throat).*
> Therapist: Are you saying "go on" because you feel you're able to agree, or are you saying "go on" for some other reason?
> Patient: I'm saying "go on" 'cause I guess we'll just cross that bridge if we come to it.
> Therapist: These are conditions for the conduct of the treatment, and it's very important that before we begin, we agree that there is a basis for beginning. One of the cornerstones of this work would be our ability to rely on your open and honest communication.

Comment

The therapist is very careful not to assume that the patient's "go on" signifies her agreement to the condition to speak freely, and therefore he pursues clarification of the meaning of that phrase. This clarification shows that the patient is taking the position that obstacles to the treatment ought to be taken up only after the treatment has started (or that she is treating the discussion of the conditions of treatment as irrelevant and is just trying to get into treatment). While it is appropriate to defer full discussion of most issues until later in the treatment, the interviewer is emphasizing that for the therapeutic work to take place it is necessary first to establish minimal agreed-upon guidelines.

> Patient: I understand the purpose of . . . of . . . of doing it, of saying it. I'm just not so sure that I'll be able to. I'm not saying that I'm not going to try. I'll give it a try.
> Therapist: Mmm hmm.
> Patient: There's a big difference between committing myself to something that I'm not so sure I can do. I don't want to lie and say, "Yes, I will definitely say everything that's on my mind," because right now I'm not saying everything that's on my mind, so how can I tell you that in three weeks or in four weeks I'll be able to do that?
> Therapist: What I need to know at this point is that whatever is

on your mind that you're not saying does not bear on the issues that we're discussing.

Comment

Again, the interviewer indicates an appreciation that the task of being a responsible patient is difficult. Notwithstanding this appreciation of the difficulties, however, the clinician is not a magician who can make do with less than the minimum requirements. Hence, despite an appreciation that the patient may not be able to speak freely on every topic at this point, the therapist must be clear that the patient's comments on contract-setting issues reflect a full awareness of her thoughts and feelings.

PATIENT: What I'm not saying right now isn't bearing on this issue. As far as this issue goes, I can just tell you I can make every effort to do what you're asking . . . it's going to be hard.

THERAPIST: Yes, it is very hard. Now, in terms of discussing my responsibilities: first, I will be responsible to the schedule we will work out. If, for any reason, I am unable to make a session, and generally I would know that a month in advance, I would give you that information. Whenever that occurs, I will also try to reschedule the appointment.

PATIENT: Well, what kind of situation do you think would prevent you from coming to therapy?

THERAPIST: Apart from regularly scheduled events, such as vacations or professional meetings, only emergency situations that I could not predict in advance. Barring those, my responsibility is to be here just as is yours. In other words, we share equally our responsibility. *(Pause)* Beyond that my effort will be to try to understand your communication, which I may not always be able to do fully, and to comment when I feel it is useful. There may be situations where you expect me to talk or answer your questions when I do not. You may even have reactions, occasionally strong reactions, or assumptions about why I did not speak. Therefore, you should know in advance that I will be guided by what I feel is useful for you, which may not in every instance be the same as what you feel is useful.

Comment

The interviewer signals appreciation that the patient might well expect a different response from the therapist than what might occur. Indeed, the basis for the interviewer's explanation at this point is that the patient is entitled to be told of the therapist's behavior because it might fly in the face of what the patient's common sense might predict.

> PATIENT: When you talk about those "strong reactions," what if I get really upset? When I got really upset, my old therapist used to hug me. If I asked him for a hug, he'd give me a hug. Are you going to do that?
>
> THERAPIST: No, I will not. This is a talking treatment. There will be no physical contact, though I understand that you have a history with your previous therapist that would lead you to expect that.

Comment

Patients' expectations are often based on their prior therapeutic experience as well as their common sense. It is essential that the interviewer clarify that the patient's prior experience, which understandably might lead her to expect similar patterns of behavior in the future, will not be repeated, if that is the case.

> PATIENT: That's going to be hard to adjust to . . .
>
> THERAPIST: Mmm hmm.
>
> PATIENT: . . . 'cause I found it helpful.
>
> THERAPIST: Mmm hmm.
>
> PATIENT: Comforting.
>
> THERAPIST: Mmm hmm.
>
> PATIENT: And may . . . and kind of made it easier to talk about those things that maybe I didn't want to talk about.
>
> THERAPIST: Mmm hmm. *(Pause)* Well, if *(pause)* the question is whether I'm willing to barter with you, your open and honest communication in exchange for my hugs, let me reinforce what I said a minute ago. This is a talking treatment, and there will be no physical contact between us, which is a departure from your previous treatment. *(Pause)*

Comment

The patient, in pleading her case, has moved from a simple complaint that it would be difficult to follow the rules to the suggestion that the therapeutic process would improve if the interviewer agreed to deviate from what he has presented as a nonnegotiable issue. If the patient had said this after treatment had begun, then it would be important to explore fully the transference implications of her movement away from entreaty and into challenge, but in this phase the issue is whether a climate can be created that will permit such exploration to take place. The interviewer treats the patient's remark in a straightforward manner, first identifying it, and then matter-of-factly re-emphasizing his earlier position.

> THERAPIST: Speaking of your previous treatment, there were two issues that you brought up in the sessions we had preceding this one that seemed to me to be crucial for us to discuss at this point because potentially they pose a considerable threat to the treatment. I want to establish now what the ground rules will be about those two issues in order to see whether we have a basis for going on. You made me aware that in the past you've made four or five suicide attempts, and that your previous therapists, as I recall, responded to those attempts in a more or less similar fashion. They were continually available to you by phone, would go with you to the emergency room if you asked them to, and on at least one occasion admitted you to their hospital and treated you in the hospital. As with the hugging, I can understand that you may have an expectation that I will act in a similar fashion. So I want to now make clear what my position is, and then we can discuss whether this position is acceptable to you.

Comment

The interviewer reviews in detail the patient's past experiences, indicating both that an appreciation of why the patient might anticipate similar behavior in the future and, precisely for that reason, why the therapist must explicate how this treatment needs to be conducted with regard to these issues. Note that the interviewer begins the transition to the next set of parameters by informing the patient that after this position is presented, they can discuss whether it is "acceptable to you." The interviewer is emphasizing that the patient is free to agree or not to the interviewer's conditions. However, the interviewer is not free to change the rules since they represent the minimum conditions necessary for the conduct of the treatment.

The particular stance that the interviewer takes here is dictated by the information presented in the preceding history-taking sessions. The patient's history is one of multiple suicide attempts, which led previous therapists first to become actively involved in taking care of her but then to end the treatment. Specifically, the patient repeatedly acted out anger in the transference through suicidal activity, and the more the therapists involved themselves in the caretaking aspects secondary to the suicide attempts, the more hopelessly entangled the treatment became. As the therapists became more involved in the patient's life outside of sessions, they were less able to reflect from a neutral position on the material within the sessions. The therapists were drawn from a position of helping the patient observe the complex transference object she had created in the therapy to becoming real objects in the patient's life. In each instance, this led to the therapist's discontinuing the treatment. Here, the interviewer is attempting to set up a situation with the patient in which they would be able to examine in words all of the patient's feelings and thoughts. It is a good sign that the patient is asking all of these questions. Her response indicates that though she is interested in testing the limits of the interviewer's position, by the same token she takes his words seriously.

> THERAPIST: Should you become suicidal between our appointments then I would expect the following of you: First, that if you had a suicidal thought or feeling and felt you could contain it till our next session, you would do nothing except bring it up as the very first business at our next meeting. If you felt you couldn't wait, that you had an overwhelming urge to kill yourself, it would be your responsibility to go to the emergency room and be evaluated. If the evaluation there was that you needed to be admitted to the hospital, then you would be admitted to the hospital and cared for by the staff of that hospital.

PATIENT: A regular hospital?

THERAPIST: Whatever hospital was necessary to handle your particular problem. It might be a psychiatric ward in a general hospital or it might be a psychiatric hospital. The judgment would be left to the emergency room doctor. I would have no say about what happened to you once you went to the emergency room beyond providing information if asked for it and if you consented to my giving it. Under no circumstance would I involve myself until the doctor in charge of your case decided that you could resume outpatient treatment, in which case you would contact me and we would continue. If at any point you felt unable to carry through on this plan and felt compelled to involve me in some way, such as, for example, calling me and telling me that you were about to kill yourself, I would remind you of your responsibilities within our therapy to seek appropriate help. If you refused to do so, I would arrange for your admission to a hospital and, at that point, terminate the treatment. *(Long pause)*

PATIENT: It's pretty harsh. *(Long pause)* What if I call you . . . what if I've already taken something? I would still go through the same procedure? Call the hospital, not you?

THERAPIST: That's correct.

PATIENT: It just seems a little bit indirect. How can they help me more than you can? You're my doctor, not them.

THERAPIST: I'm not your doctor at the point at which you act on your impulse. At that point, this kind of treatment, which, as I mentioned earlier, is an effort to understand you through words, can no longer go on because you have chosen to act instead of talk. This is not a treatment for all situations. It is a treatment of a very specific sort for a limited kind of situation, and rather than my being harsh, it would be you who are making it impossible to continue the treatment.

Comment

This is an especially important intervention. The interviewer clarifies the limitations of this treatment approach and, based on those limitations, what can and cannot take place. Frequently, borderline patients attempt to put therapists in the role of omnipotent providers who can and must fulfill their impossible demands. Therapists who are susceptible to such entreaties are likely to feel guilty and ashamed when they recognize that the task that they have agreed to is impossible. This can lead to "heroic" attempts to provide omnipotent care, which foster the patient's unrealistic transference rather than confront her with the limits of reality. The diagnostician is not saying that the patient is not allowed to wish for around-the-clock back-up and support, but only that this is not what this therapist can offer, or recommend, and indeed is not what the patient has allegedly sought by coming for exploratory treatment.

PATIENT: If you say so.

THERAPIST: It's because one can't both talk and act at the same time. There would be no way for us to study what goes into your wish to kill yourself or, for that matter, who it is you're trying to kill, if you became involved, and expected me to become involved, in those actions. We can continue to examine what went into a particular act once your situation is stabilized. This treatment is designed to understand you through looking at your impulses and cannot be conducted if you're living them out with me.

PATIENT: So you're just interested in my talking behavior?

THERAPIST: No, I'm interested in talking about and understanding your behavior as well as your thoughts, feelings, wishes, and fears.

PATIENT: What if I had this impulse and our session isn't for days?

THERAPIST: You would have two choices: either to contain the impulse and perhaps even reflect on it yourself so that work goes on between sessions; or, if you felt you could not do that, to proceed with the options I outlined to either take yourself to an emergency room . . .

PATIENT: *(Interrupting)* Mmm hmm.

THERAPIST: . . . or, if you wished to break the contract and end our therapy, to call me. Given the history that you've presented in the first several sessions, there is a very real probability that you will be tempted to destroy and/or flee from the treatment, which is precisely why we're going through this at this point.

Comment

The interviewer emphasizes that these recommendations are based on the patient's own previous experiences, as she has reported them. The interviewer is saying, "We must learn from your experiences so as to profit from them." The borderline patient commonly holds the position that she is the victim of an arbitrary or capricious therapist. The interviewers' ability to root their interventions in the patient's prior experiences permits them, should the therapy begin, to be able later to interpret the patient's projective identifications with a comment such as: "Though you're now saying I am acting in a harsh and punitive way to fill my own needs, let me remind you that we discussed all of this in the contract setting. At that time you agreed that we had to protect the treatment from that part of you that had successfully destroyed several past efforts. I wonder what is making you forget those discussions now?"

PATIENT: C.Y.A.

THERAPIST: C.Y.A? What does that mean?

PATIENT: Covering your ass.

THERAPIST: So you . . . you see this as self serving? That raises an interesting point. I am doing what I feel is in the best interest of the treatment, or putting it slightly differently, the only way that I know to conduct this form of treatment is to protect the possibility of our understanding you against the predictable onslaught of your action. It is also true that I think it's very important that you understand that you can't destroy me. What you call "covering my ass" I would define as my effort to feel comfortable about what I'm doing so as to be able to maximally feel free to pay attention to you, as well as not worry about myself. (Pause) You may successfully commit suicide, and it would be important for you to understand that, should that happen, my life would go on much as it has before. In fact, given your history, should you agree to participate in what I think is going to be a very difficult effort to try to make sense out of your life, I would want to meet with your family as well so that everyone is clear about where I stand in relation to the possibility of your killing yourself. This meeting would address the real possibility that you may, at some point, kill yourself, as well as the degree your killing yourself could be based on a wish to harm me. A therapy in which your actions pose the least risk to me is one in which you stand to gain the most. If I am threatened, I cannot think clearly. *(Long pause)*

Comment

Note that the interviewer in no way apologizes for this position of self-preservation, a stance that is especially significant for borderline patients whose grandiosity frequently is expressed by their belief that the therapist exists solely to do the patient's bidding. Indeed, the patient's objections to the contract may come less from its specific conditions than from her need to maintain a position of narcissistic entitlement and control. An interviewer who is unclear about the necessity of creating a protected environment for the therapy to take place will be vulnerable to responding defensively to the patient's accusations. Should interviewers feel that they can or must save the patient, they will be tempted either to ignore the prior treatment experiences or to see them as a challenge, believing that they alone can do what others have failed to accomplish. The more the patient successfully appeals to the interviewer's grandiosity (an early projective identification), the more reasonable the patient's assertions will appear to be.

PATIENT: Mmm hmm.

THERAPIST: There are many issues that you've brought up that I have treated in a matter-of-fact manner because we are meeting now to see if we will be able to work together. If this were therapy, then we would have looked differently at some of the things that have come up today. For example, your tone of voice when you spoke about my covering my ass sounded cynical and accusatory. These attitudes, to the extent that I'm correct about them, would be just the sort of thing that we would be examining together over the course of this treatment. *(Pause)* If you have any more questions about that, we can discuss it. Otherwise, I want to raise one other issue that your history brought up that poses a threat to the treatment.

PATIENT: Go ahead.

THERAPIST: You've mentioned that in each of your previous therapies you missed many sessions. As I recall, you said that with
two of your therapists you came when you felt like it, and when
you weren't feeling good, you didn't show up. What you would
be agreeing to here is to come to sessions twice a week irrespective of how you feel. In fact, it may be that the times when you
feel least like coming are the most important times to come.

PATIENT: Again you're asking me to promise something that's
very hard for me. When I feel really bad, but when I feel *really*
bad, I don't do anything. It's not that I just don't come to
therapy. I don't do anything.

THERAPIST: For us to work together you would have to be prepared to come when you feel bad, even if there is nothing else
that you do that day. Because if you're not here, nothing can
happen in your therapy. It's only by our meeting regularly,
independent of your particular feeling state, that we can, over
time, develop an understanding of you. In that way we can
establish a profile of your behavior—for example, what sets you
off, how you've handled these issues in the past—and develop
alternatives for the future. But, if you are not here, then we lose
the opportunity to study that experience and learn from it.
(Pause) It's not I who's asking you to do the impossible; it's you
who's asking me to do so, because it's impossible for me to treat
you if you are not here. Yet your tone and your words seem to
suggest that it is I who is imposing an unfair burden on you.

Comment

The interviewer does not take up the issue of what the patient is or isn't
able to do, but focuses only on what is required for the conduct of the
treatment. It does not matter why the patient would be unable to come
to sessions. The essential fact remains that without her participation,
treatment is impossible. Yet the patient is demanding that her needs
require the clinician to circumvent reality. Interviewers do not say that
they require the patient's attendance at session, but that the *treatment*
requires it, that they are unable to conduct treatment by themselves.

PATIENT: Well, in a way it is. I mean you're unfair. You're illogical because you're. . . . How can I say, "Yes I will come to every session?" If I'm not feeling well, I'm not feeling well!

THERAPIST: I would assume that if you were feeling well you would not be needing therapy. You have sought my help precisely because you're not feeling well. As I mentioned a moment ago, my ability to help you is contingent upon your being here.

PATIENT: I'll try.

THERAPIST: I'm concerned about this point, given your previous history. My sense is that you not only question your ability to come but also my sincerity. You think that perhaps I don't really mean what I am saying about the necessity for you to keep the appointments?

Comment

The combination of the patient's experience with prior therapists, her own grandiosity, and the pseudo-acquiescence suggested by her "I'll try" lead the interviewer to wonder whether the patient understands that the decision to enter the treatment phase is a function of what happens during the contract setting. The therapist considers the possibility that she may be giving lip service to the conditions of the contract in order to get beyond these "formalities" and engage in therapy just as she has always done before.

PATIENT: Going back to what you were talking about before with the suicide, you seem like a hard ass.

THERAPIST: So, it's clear to you that I do mean this?

PATIENT: Yeah. I'm just not all that sure about my half. I'm sure you can perform your part of the deal.

THERAPIST: Only if you perform your part of the deal. We either do this together or not at all. I get the sense there are two discussions going on here. One has to do with the particular issues that I'm raising with you—for example, suicide attempts and how they would be handled, and missing appointments. The other has to do with the more general issue that I'm making demands of you. You seem to find that offensive, as if, how dare I ask this of you?

PATIENT: I don't have anything to say.

Comment

At this point, instead of focusing on the issue of making demands on the patient, interviewers could alternatively suggest that what threatens the patient is their statement that therapists have limitations. If the interviewer were omnipotent, nothing would be required of the patient. By the same token, if the patient were omnipotent, she would be able to extract from the interviewer anything she wished and, therefore, would be able to compel the interviewer to set up a no-conditions treatment. The contract challenges the patient's belief in her capacity for omnipotent control and her complementary wish for an omnipotent other, cardinal features of most borderline patients.

THERAPIST: Does that mean that nothing comes to mind or does that mean, as you said at the beginning, that there are things that you won't say, or might not be able to say?

PATIENT: Nothing comes to mind.

THERAPIST: So I take that to mean that you are in agreement on all points?

PATIENT: With some trepidation, but it's like kicking a dead horse.

THERAPIST: What does that mean?

PATIENT: It means going over the same stuff. I don't feel that much different about what you're telling me than I did five minutes ago.

THERAPIST: If you were me, what would you take your last statement to signify regarding your agreeing to your responsibilities?

PATIENT: I'm not sure I understand what you mean.

THERAPIST: You said you feel the same as you did five minutes ago. So I'm asking you, if you were me, how should I hear that comment?

PATIENT: That I'm still having a bit of a problem with the framework you want me to work in.

THERAPIST: We should continue to talk about that.

PATIENT: It's very constraining. I'm supposed to say "yes" to you, but wanting to kill myself is a very strong feeling. Coming to therapy is a different kind of thing. You talk like they're part and parcel of each other, but they're two separate things. Trying to kill myself is a serious thing; not coming to therapy is not coming to therapy.

THERAPIST: The way I would join the two is that each of them has a potential for murdering the treatment. *(Pause.)* From the point of view of our ability to do work, killing yourself or not showing up makes therapy impossible. In either case, you will have succeeded in indulging that part of you that, by history, has already successfully destroyed several treatment efforts. What we are attempting to do, and when I say "we" I mean myself and that part of you that is seeking help, is to protect the treatment from the part of you that wishes to destroy the very thing you're coming here for. And, as I mentioned to you, I sensed that you were offering me a swap, as if these points could be negotiated. I want to reiterate again that there can be no flexibility about these points. For us to work, you need to be here. Your fantasy of me is that I believe it is easy for you to follow this prescription. If we agree to work together, we could discuss your fantasy, but that's separate and distinct from this arrangement.

Comment

The patient's alleging that the therapist is insensitive to her difficulty ("Aren't I the patient? How can you ask anything of me?") is the continued expression of her insistence that nothing should be required of her. The patient focuses exclusively on the primacy of her needs as if that obligates the therapist to surmount any obstacle and to modify the necessary conditions for treatment. At this point the therapist offers an empathic comment showing an awareness of how difficult it will be for this patient truly to engage in therapy. Note that the therapist maintains the boundary between the contract setting and the therapy; *if* they agree to proceed with therapy, they will be able to explore her fantasy that the therapist does not appreciate how difficult therapy will be for her.

PATIENT: If I say, "Yeah, okay I agree," then therapy begins?

THERAPIST: If you say it and mean it, yes. I sense that these issues are not firmly resolved in your mind. I suggest we spend the next session continuing to discuss them, at the end of which we will decide whether or not to begin the treatment. We have to stop for now.

PATIENT: Okay.

Summary

The contract-setting session just presented is generally adequate, though it is incomplete and will have to be followed up in the next session. While the therapist's work in this session proceeds at a pace that is determined by the interaction with the patient, the therapist keeps in mind throughout the contract-setting process the three different content areas reviewed in the first part of this chapter: patient responsibilities; therapist responsibilities; and predicted threats to the treatment.

An important aspect of this stage of the therapeutic dialogue is that, coming right after the history taking, it is the first interactive opportunity between patient and therapist and is, therefore, the initial exposure the patient has to the therapist's attitude toward her problems and the work of therapy. Does the therapist takes her seriously? Does the therapist mean what he or she says? Is the therapist respectful? Does he or she show evidence of a willingness to give and take? The initial interactions will offer the patient preliminary answers to these questions. Timing is an important element in this process; therapists use their clinical judgment to decide when to introduce and pursue each different aspect of the contract, and they try to discuss them in a way that emphasizes that they are linked to underlying principles and are not simply a list of "do's" and "don't's."

The patient's responsibilities—especially those involving attendance and payment—may, at first, seem elementary and self-evident, not requiring extensive discussion. However, one must keep in mind that a patient can express resistance around any detail of the parameters of treatment. Since resistance, particularly in borderline patients, may be linked with highly destructive forces, it is important to take note of it as soon as any evidence emerges. In the session just presented, the patient, after mild opposition at first, appears to agree to the expectation around attendance. However, later in the session the therapist returns to the issue because of the patient's history of irregular attendance. At that point the patient's resistance comes through more strongly; and the therapist must clearly state that if she does not attend regularly, she will make it impossible to carry out the treatment. By perceiving and challenging the patient's projection onto the therapist of a demanding and unreasonable authoritarian voice, the therapist can point out that she is the one who is putting unreasonable demands on the therapy.

Since even the most concrete and apparently clear-cut detail of the therapy can become the arena for the projection of important intrapsychic dynamics, it is essential to assess carefully the responses of the patient. The therapist strives to maintain a position of alertness to any evidence—verbal or behavioral—of disagreement in the patient, while avoiding obsessive, insensitive belaboring of the need for agreement (see the first case study in chapter 6). The therapist's curiosity in pursuing a patient's disagreement with a specific aspect of the contract can help in the early delineation of dynamic patterns that may represent central intrapsychic paradigms of the patient (see chapter 7).

CHAPTER 4

Setting Up the Contract: Common Problems

SETTING UP THE CONTRACT is a critical part of the therapeutic process. Its elaboration represents a microcosm of the dynamics that will unfold in the treatment. Because of this, the therapist must appreciate the complexities that can develop around establishing the contract, avoid treating the contract setting prematurely as therapy, and keep in mind the particular techniques of the contract-setting phase—repeated clarification of the conditions of treatment and of the patient's response to these conditions.

Inadequate Presentation of the Contract

The problems a therapist might encounter in setting up the contract vary from the simple and easily remedied to the more complicated issues of projection and countertransference. The simplest problems stem from therapists' not having adequately familiarized themselves with the principles and details of contract-setting. The therapist may skip over or superficially refer to one or more of the tripartite divisions of the contract—patient responsibilities, therapist responsibilities, and threats to the treatment—or to a component of one of these areas—for example, conditions around attendance or missed sessions. It is not necessary for the therapist to address the different parts of the contract in the order presented here. Some therapists first discuss those aspects concerning potential threats to the treatment since these issues have entered the dialogue in the history-taking sessions.

Problems in Pursuing
the Patient's Response

An intermediate form of problem would arise if the therapist did an adequate job in terms of presenting the conditions of treatment in each area, but then failed to explore adequately the patient's response. This type of error is extremely common since patients often reply with a superficial compliance, saying little or nothing about their real thoughts. A superficial response, such as "That sounds OK to me," should be explored to make sure that the patient actually heard, took in, and considered the words of the therapist; the therapist might say, "Could you tell me your understanding of the conditions you are agreeing to?"

At this point in the process of setting up the contract, therapists might typically err in one of two ways. They might be reluctant to pursue the patient's understanding, fearing that exploration would elicit underlying objection or anger from the patient. Fear of the patient's objecting to the terms of treatment is often based on therapists' concern that the patient might, in fact, not accept the treatment being offered. This concern is most typical of beginning therapists, who often judge their success or failure by whether they "kept or lost" the patient. It is important that therapists keep in mind that the most essential part of the work at this stage is to establish conditions of treatment that will allow exploratory therapy to happen. It does not help the patient to participate in a treatment whose frame (or lack thereof) allows her to continue to avoid experiencing the conflicts and affects that are at the root of her maladaptive behaviors. Some authors would argue that it is most important to meet patients "where they are" and to work from there. In our experience, borderline patients, whose histories are replete with multiple failed treatments, often show that they are able to comply with expectations even though they, and their previous therapists, had thought they were incapable of accepting these responsibilities.

In addition to the concern that the patient might not accept the treatment, therapists might be wary that uncovering strong objections to the conditions of the contract would open the "Pandora's box" of the negative transference. It is essential to keep in mind the role of transference and countertransference issues during the contract-setting phase, especially since the very term "contract" suggests a fundamentally cognitive process, possibly distracting therapists from the dynamic issues involved. Yet the difficulties that typically surface during contract setting illustrate how even the most cognitive/rational element of the treatment can become a field in which intrapsychic dynamics are played out. From this point of view it could be argued that an entire therapy might revolve around the discussion of the conditions of treatment; this would focus the treatment on transference issues quickly without involving anamnesis in a major role in the therapy. This approach may not be close to the current training of most therapists; therefore, the emphasis in this book will be on awareness of transference and countertransference within the contract-setting process, without developing that process as the major arena for the ongoing work of the therapy. Thus, while an awareness of these issues is important to guide their interventions during this phase of treatment, it is recommended that therapists keep interpretation to a minimum and emphasize clarification with appropriate confrontation of inconsistencies. To shift the focus to interpretation now would suggest that the therapist has already begun to view the work with the patient as an ongoing therapy, thus transgressing the boundary between the evaluation/contract-setting phase and the exploratory therapy per se.

As for the therapists who fear encountering major objections to the conditions of the contract, because these therapists may sense the potential for an angry and devaluing response from the patient they may shy away from any exploration or confrontation. This would be an error on two scores. First, they would be working under the illusion that they could control what comes out of the patient. This would be an illusion not only because therapists cannot exert this type of control, but also because in this case it would be the patients who are controlling the therapists' behavior in the session. The second problem is that the therapists are attempting to avoid the emergence of the negative transference. Transference, and countertransference, begin to emerge very early in the therapy of these patients. Working with the negative transference is essential in the treatment of borderline patients. In our experience, the sooner the negative transference emerges in the treatment, and the sooner it is made clear that it can be contained in the treatment, the more likely the treatment is to continue and to get at the central issues.

Therapists who are at the stage of pursuing the patient's response to the conditions of the contract could err in the opposite direction: Instead of avoiding exploration of the patient's response, they might address the patient with a tenacity and assiduousness that take on an aggressive quality of their own. The therapists might begin by appropriately inquiring about the patient's response; however, once this had been explored, they might continue to ask again and again for further reactions from the patient and further assurances that she indeed understands and accepts the contract. This situation is an example of how any material that comes up in therapy, whatever its manifest content, can be used in a defensive manner by either the therapist or the patient. In this case, the therapist may already be caught up in a projective identification and may be acting out, through bearing down on the patient, aggression originating in the patient. The therapists could also be enacting aggression of their own, whether it be primary or in reaction to anxiety evoked by the prospect of working with a potentially difficult patient. Therapists are not immune to blindness regarding their own resistance around accepting a case and their subsequent actions that may contribute to the patient's leaving treatment. Attention to the treatment contract, meant to strengthen and advance the treatment, could turn into overbearingness and become the arena in which a therapist's ambivalence gets played out. Thus, the therapists' attention must be directed as much to their own participation in the contract-setting process as to the patient's. If therapists have reservations about treating a particular patient, or borderline patients in general, they should address this issue directly and avoid turning the contract-setting process into a way to dispatch an unwelcome patient. One of the main reasons for the focus on the treatment contract is the need to make the therapy feel safe enough to therapists so that they are not subject to this kind of anxiety.

Difficulties Stemming from
Unclarity of Approach to Borderline Patients

A somewhat more complicated form of difficulty with the contract occurs when therapists have adequately studied the contract-setting procedure and are able to carry it out in its complexity, but inwardly harbor objections to it as a technique of therapy. These objections could be based on an honest difference of opinion with this approach to treatment, in which case therapists should refrain from applying it. On the other hand, the objections could be based on countertransference issues with regard to the whole category of borderline patients. For example, a therapist might feel that borderline patients are unfairly scapegoated as difficult patients; thus any special focus on setting up their contracts perpetuates this scapegoating, humiliating the patient by "requiring" her to agree to a particularly rigid treatment frame.

Another example of countertransference would be therapists who saw borderline patients as so marked by constitutional deficit that the demands of the contract were unrealistic: "If the patient could follow these expectations, they wouldn't need therapy . . . they'd be at the end of their treatment." Of course, the establishment of the treatment contract is a challenging task. It requires skill on the part of the therapist and effort by the patient to agree to responsibilities she may never have accepted before. Yet therapists who feel that the demands of the contract are unrealistic for the patient might wonder about their anxiety with regard to setting up an expectation or limit with patients who are renowned for impulsive, rageful reactions. The most complex problems that arise around the setting up of the contract occur in cases where the therapists have done a thorough job of presenting the contract and have carefully begun to assess the patient's reaction but then begin to *undo* some of their work because of countertransference feelings and cannot adhere to the task as planned. We will examine this situation in more detail. Countertransference problems occur when the therapists' knowledge of what to do is interfered with by feelings provoked in them that lead to changing course in midstream.

It is important to keep in mind that the treatment plan, which at this point is setting up a contract for expressive therapy, is predicated on an adequate diagnostic impression. Before beginning to set up the

81

contract, the therapist should be comfortable that the patient is organized at a borderline level (Kernberg, 1977.) If, in setting up the contract with a patient, therapists begin to change course because of emerging doubts that the patient may be psychotic, this would not necessarily be a problem with the countertransference. An appropriate technique at that point would be to reassess the diagnostic question, holding in abeyance the establishment of the contract until this question is resolved. If, however, the therapists acted on their doubts about diagnosis by changing the conditions being set up *as if* those doubts immediately required a change in the conditions of the contract, they would be at risk of acting out the countertransference. A more therapeutic approach would be to examine their reaction, as well as the emerging picture of the patient, to see what further information about the patient's inner world of affects and object relations can be ascertained.

The importance of the diagnostic impression cannot be overestimated since these patients may be subject to brief psychotic episodes and also to episodes of transference psychosis. Some of the most difficult moments later on in the treatment may involve understanding and dealing with such phenomena. These eventualities bear directly on issues of contract setting since the expectations of the contract imply that the patient is able to take responsibility for herself rather than shift it to someone else. Questions about the emergence of psychosis are among the strongest pressures the therapist may experience to deviate from the conditions of the contract.

Case Example

The following example involves a therapist who has done an adequate job setting up the contract, but who then begins to waver. The therapist has gone through the contract to the point of addressing the specific threats to the treatment this patient presents by virtue of her history and behavior in the evaluation sessions. The patient has been in three prior therapies. Those therapies were characterized by her difficulty in openly discussing her feelings in sessions and by her frequent calls to the therapist between sessions when she felt "overwhelmed" and suicidal. Her suicidal feelings were often precipitated by crises in her relationships with boyfriends. Each therapy ended when the patient was hospitalized because of an intensification of suicidal feelings, at which time each therapist recommended to the inpatient team that the patient have a fresh start with a new therapist upon discharge.

What follows is from the fifth session. In the first three sessions, the therapist reviewed the patient's history and established her impression of the diagnosis. In the fourth session the therapist presented the parts of the contract involving general patient and therapist responsibilities within the treatment.

THERAPIST: I'd like to address now the issue of your suicidal behaviors and how they interfered with the course of your therapies in the past and the conditions I would propose to minimize the likelihood that those behaviors will interfere with the treatment we are considering beginning here.

PATIENT: OK.

THERAPIST: Your prior therapist reports, and you pretty much agree with him, that every time you began to talk about the questions you have about whether your father might have abused you sexually—whenever you began to wonder if you were beginning to get in touch with real memories, or if those were fantasies or dreams—you began to report being overwhelmed by suicidal urges. You would call your therapist in the evening to tell him that the session had made you increasingly upset and that you weren't sure if you could make it through the night without hurting yourself. You would imply, or sometimes say, that it was his interest in these questions of possible sexual abuse that made you go into those thoughts more deeply than you could tolerate. He would agree to talk with you on the phone until you felt calm enough to go to bed, and if talking on the phone didn't seem to be helping, he would agree to meet you at the emergency room where you could be evaluated for admission.

PATIENT: He thought that was the safest plan, and I think he was right, because I'm still here to tell the story, and if it hadn't been for him, I might have wound up dead one of those nights.

THERAPIST: That's one way to look at it. On the other hand, it sounds like that therapy ended because you and your therapist agreed that it was going nowhere. At best, as you say, it was keeping you alive. But after two years of treatment your therapist felt that any efforts to help you increase your understanding of your problems and your control over them was stymied.

PATIENT: He had his limits. I decided to start treatment with you because I heard you specialize in the kind of problems I have, so I knew I could trust you to take care of me.

THERAPIST: Well, first of all, I have to remind you that we haven't started treatment yet; we're still talking about the conditions of treatment which would apply if we work together. If we agree on that, then we can begin. But I would suggest that your certainty that I will "take care of you" is exactly the problem we're discussing with regard to your prior therapy. It seems that you saw your therapy with Dr. Smith as a relationship where he would take care of you and where your only responsibility was to call him when you were upset, thus activating his intervention.

PATIENT: That wasn't my only responsibility. I was also responsible for coming to sessions and saying what was on my mind.

THERAPIST: But we have to look more closely at that because it sounds like you came to sessions and then didn't always follow through with reporting what was on your mind.

PATIENT: I don't know what you're talking about. The whole point that you started talking about today is that when I *did* talk about what was on my mind, I couldn't deal with it and needed extra help.

THERAPIST: I could imagine that when you did begin to discuss your ideas about the possibility of having been sexually abused that you didn't follow through with saying everything that came to mind. It sounds like those sessions were accompanied by very strong feelings of confusion, despair, and rage, and yet what I hear about those sessions is that when you began to talk about sexual abuse, you would shut down and spend the rest of the session is silence.

PATIENT: I couldn't cope with the feelings. You can't ask me to do something I can't do.

THERAPIST: While it's true that I can't determine what you can and can't do, I can tell you what is necessary for this therapy to have

84

a chance of working. It is necessary for you to report what you are feeling with regard to the problems that brought you into treatment. If, at any given point, you feel overwhelmed with feelings that keep you from continuing to discuss what you were talking about, then it is your responsibility to try to describe those overwhelming feelings since they represent the main problem at hand. If we are to work together, it will have to be with the understanding that our communication will be limited to scheduled session times and that, barring true emergencies, you will not call me between sessions.

PATIENT: But if my feeling suicidal isn't a true emergency, what is?

THERAPIST: Your suicidality unfortunately does not have the characteristics of an emergency since it is a chronic condition you have been living with for years. We have discussed that. We have discussed the option of hospitalization rather than outpatient therapy at this point and have agreed that such a plan would only offer relative safety for the short term. There would not be time in the hospital for you to make the major internal changes—the changes in the way you look at yourself and the world—that you need to make in order to get beyond the chronic risk of suicide. Therefore, the main options are either the kind of therapy we are talking about, which could lead to long-term change, but which does entail the risk that you might act on your suicidal impulses before you gain more control over them, or a custodial form of hospitalization, which would provide relative, though not complete, safety but which would keep you isolated from functioning in the world and would limit your possibilities of exploring your problems and adapting and advancing in life. You, and your family, have decided that the outpatient approach makes more sense. I agree with that, but only under the condition that you see this treatment as one in which you maintain responsibility for yourself. Therefore, when you say that you came to seek treatment with me because you "knew you could trust me to take care of you," I have to stop and focus the discussion on this issue of responsibility. My view of therapy is to help you work on your problems. My responsibility is to see that the therapy we are engaged in is appropriate for you and is done properly. That does not guarantee that you will overcome your problems and does not put the responsibility for your actions and your life in my hands. It does not make me a case manager, a decision maker, or a substitute for the other supports you may need to live your life and get some gratification from it. In the course of treatment, you may want to examine why you have a history of alienating those supports, but that is different from my taking the place of those supports in your life. Is that description of the issue of my responsibility within the therapy clear to you?

PATIENT: Yes.

THERAPIST: Are you interested in hearing more about what the treatment would be like?

PATIENT: Yes.

THERAPIST: A major obstacle to the success of your last therapy seemed to be the fact that you would stop talking in sessions and then call your therapist at night, as we discussed earlier. I want to make it clear that my offering you therapy here does not mean that I will be available around-the-clock to talk with you over the phone. This is for three reasons. The first is that the option of the phone calls may have contributed to your shutting down in sessions. The second is that I do not feel that the work of therapy can be done over the phone, and I do not see how phone calls would serve any purpose except in the case of true emergencies. The third reason is that I cannot realistically be available on an around-the-clock basis, and it would be dangerous for you to erroneously believe that I was offering that availability.

PATIENT: Okay . . . I understand what you're saying, and I guess I'll have to take my chances (pause).

THERAPIST: What do you mean exactly by "take your chances"?

PATIENT: I mean, you're right . . . it is an uncertain game. I've blown it in my therapies so far, and this time I have to take some chances. When you get right down to it, I think you and I agree more than we realized at first. You're saying there are no guarantees, and I guess I've really thought that all along myself. It's been kind of reassuring to think those other guys could keep me safe in therapy, but I guess it hasn't been real. I could use a dose of reality now; I'm ready to go for broke. If it works, it works.

If it doesn't, it doesn't . . . but at least I can say I tried the real thing. I like your serious approach to therapy, and I guess that's the most important thing—to think you've done the work right. That *is* more important than the outcome.

Comment

The therapist has done a good job in this part of the contract setting. She has explicitly addressed the following issues: 1) the fact that the therapy has not begun, and cannot begin until and unless an agreement is reached about the conditions of treatment; 2) predicted threats to the treatment—the patient's suicidality, her withholding during session, and her calls between sessions; 3) the distinction between a true emergency and the chronic ongoing risk of suicide; 4) the nature of the responsibility of the therapist and of the patient to the treatment; 5) the fact that this kind of therapy cannot be carried out if certain basic conditions are not agreed to; and 6) the rules about phone calls that will apply in the treatment. She has also implicitly addressed the issues of idealization/devaluation and omnipotent control. The patient has brought up some mild objections along the way but has generally been cooperative and accepted the therapist's point of view.

However, a more complicated process has begun with the patient's last remarks. While she overtly agrees with the therapist, her remarks take on an ambivalent tone; agreement proceeds to possible irony and sarcasm. The therapist, facing a blend of overt cooperation with undertones of aggression, may begin to feel uneasy. She has been firm thus far and has carefully held to the principles of the treatment. Yet, the patient's sudden enthusiastic agreement may result in her beginning to squirm in her seat: Isn't this agreement what she has solicited? And yet it does not feel right. The therapist senses the possible mockery, but is not sure what to do with it. She begins to get angry. She has been doing her job well, and she expected either disagreement or agreement from the patient. She is not sure what to do with an apparent agreement that feels like the opposite. She is not comfortable with the anger she feels; she is afraid she might respond in a defensive or sarcastic way. Indeed, she senses, on a preconscious level, the possibility that she could become enraged, truly sadistic, toward this patient. The patient has been a challenge from the start, seemingly contesting every word the diagnostician said, and now she has made an about-face. The therapist is confused, a perfectly respectable position to be in when working with these patients—as long as she acknowledges it and takes time to think. She must remain neutral, she reminds herself. She listens to the patient, who continues:

> PATIENT: After all, who can guarantee any outcome? They laugh at that old phrase about "The operation was a success, but the patient died," but it really makes sense, and I understand you're just saying the same thing about therapy . . . and I agree with you. It's high time I got over this idea that I couldn't really kill myself and just bit the bullet. In fact, it's kind of exciting to think of this as the "make it or break it" therapy . . . with my impulses . . . but there's always a chance.

Comment

The attempted blackmail has begun. By taking the therapist's words and repeating them back to her in a way that makes the possibility of a successful outcome of the treatment seem out of the question, the patient creates a scenario where she is sacrificing herself to the purity of the treatment, a position she implies she could use as an excuse for a successful suicide: "It's not my life that counts, it's whether or not we can say we carried out a purebred treatment, for as long as it lasts."

> THERAPIST: Just a minute. I think we have to look at what you're saying. It sounds to me as if you're beginning to use the conditions of treatment I'm describing as a pretext for possibly killing yourself.
> PATIENT: Boy, I can't win with you; I was just saying how I agreed with what you're saying.
> THERAPIST: But I don't want you to take it to an extreme. After all, it's true that you could have a serious impulse in response to a real emergency.

Comment

The therapist is hooked. While a minute ago she was feeling angry, her anger has been overshadowed by doubt—doubt about the methods of the therapy she is proposing. This replacement of her anger by doubt is very likely a more complicated process than a simple reaction to the threat communicated by the patient. The clinician's burgeoning awareness of her anger may have been the principal catalyst of her doubt: Is she indeed setting limits to help the patient and the therapy, or is she just trying to protect herself from a patient she fears will be bothersome? Even worse, is she unconsciously trying to harm her? While clinicians often attribute the difficulty in working with borderline patients to the aggression coming from the patient, a far more challenging aspect of the treatment can be the aggression and sadism catalyzed in the therapist by the patient (Maltsberger & Buie, 1974).

The patient has made use of the defense of projective identification in an effort to rid herself of an uncomfortable feeling of rage that has been growing as the therapist has been describing the conditions of the treatment. She has relieved herself of this distress by responding in a way that provoked the diagnostician's rage via projection and consequent identification. The therapist's distress at beginning to feel anger and aggression in herself illustrates the challenge of working with patients who have the ability to activate the therapist's capacity for aggression.

PATIENT: You mean like my boyfriend leaving?

THERAPIST: Something like that. If it *is* an emergency, I am available for consultation over the phone . . . at a time like that it's a somewhat different ball game . . . the rules are more flexible.

Comment

The well-presented contract is beginning to falter. The therapist has begun to let the patient define the terms and conditions. Just a few minutes earlier, the therapist had made it clear that a true emergency was something unforeseen and acute (that is, a serious accident, suddenly being fired from a job, learning of the death of someone close, testing positive for HIV, or being diagnosed with cancer). She now readily accepts the idea that the patient's boyfriend's leaving would constitute an emergency. The clinician, caught up in an intrapsychic process of her own, has apparently forgotten that this patient's history is replete with boyfriends breaking up with her—such an occurrence would no more be a true emergency than the patient having a self-destructive impulse in response to any other frustration. The clinician's capacity to think clearly has been impaired by the dynamics of the situation. In addition to letting the patient be the one to define what constitutes an emergency, the therapist is speaking here as though she has forgotten what she said earlier about not being available around the clock. The therapist has lost her skills, probably through a process of projective identification that has gone unobserved and uninterpreted. It is in such a situation that a clear understanding of the contract—and the principles behind it—is especially helpful. If the therapist is monitoring her own response, she will note the deviation from the parameters of the contract. The next step is to take time to think. While this may sound like a simple step, it is often not easy in the midst of a session with a borderline patient. Any hesitation, any imperfection on the part of the therapist may become the target of devaluing remarks. The patient, even if she is angry with the therapist, probably harbors the wish that the therapist appear seamless in her presentation—a reflection of the wish for an omnipotent other whose perfection and power can fix all that is ill in the patient. The therapist feels a pressure to know all automatically, and believes she will be in trouble if she does not. Yet, the most therapeutic intervention at this point may be to say: "Something is going on here right now that I don't fully understand and that I would like to think about. Your statement of agreement with the contract seems more complicated than it appears on the surface. Before proceeding on to the therapy, I think we should explore it further."

This intervention accomplishes a number of things; in it, the therapist simultaneously: 1) shows the patient that she can empathize with the patient's state of inner confusion; 2) offers herself as a model of thoughtful reflectiveness with whom the patient may begin to identify; and 3) provides an *in vivo* demonstration of the therapist's responsibilities within the treatment—she will provide what help she can to the process of understanding, but she is not omniscient and cannot cure the patient by magic. If this intervention does, indeed, provoke a negative response from the patient ("You seem more confused than I am; maybe I should be your therapist"), the therapist can take note of this as an early manifestation of negative transference and earmark it as an area they could explore together if they enter into therapy:

It seems as though you feel one of us should be totally on top of things and the other relegated to a position of incompetence and humiliation. We could explore this view of things further if we begin therapy. For now I think we should return to trying to clarify what's going on concerning the conditions of treatment under discussion.

A rule of thumb relevant to the situation in this example is that a therapist should not change any parameter of treatment without having had adequate time to reflect on all the meanings that the change, and the urge to make the change, might represent. This often means deferring any decision on a change in parameter to the following session, and it always provides good material for supervision.

CHAPTER 5

Contracting Around Threats to the Treatment

THE PATIENT CAN experience therapy in a myriad of ways, one being as an extension of or stand-in for the more positive, health-seeking side of herself. Hence, the intrapsychic conflict pitting the self-destructive side of the patient against the usually weaker health-seeking side can be projected onto the therapeutic situation. As described in chapter 2, borderline patients often target therapy as an object of their self-destructive drives since therapy and the therapist take on roles determined by the patient's inner world of object representations.

The forms of aggressiveness and destructiveness that may be directed at the therapy vary greatly, ranging from the blunt and obvious to the indirect and subtle. Accordingly, threats to the treatment may manifest themselves in so many different forms that it is not possible to provide an exhaustive listing of them. Nor is it realistic for the therapist to expect to predict in advance all the ways a particular patient might, during the course of treatment, threaten the therapy. Nonetheless, in many cases, a review of the patient's history, her behavior in prior treatments, and her interactions during the evaluation sessions give important information concerning the most likely potential challenges. The most common threats fall into the following seven categories:

1. Suicidality
2. Homicidality
3. Problems threatening attendance or quality of participation in sessions
4. Nonlethal self-destructiveness
5. Intrusions into the therapist's personal life
6. Repeated efforts to involve the therapist in the patient's life in an active way beyond the boundaries of therapy
7. Problems created outside the sessions which would impinge on the conduct of the therapy

This list is to some degree homologous to the hierarchy of thematic priorities discussed by Kernberg and his colleagues (1989) in the chapter on "Conducting a Session" in *Psychodynamic Psychotherapy of Borderline Patients*. The hierarchy of priorities helps therapists sort out what to address when facing the overload of confusing data which so often confronts them in sessions with borderline patients. The degree to which that list of priorities coincides with our list of likely challenges to the treatment that require contracting speaks to the importance of the contract as a guiding structure throughout the life of the therapy. In this chapter we will discuss and provide examples of contracting around each of the seven threats to treatment just listed. In chapter 7 we will present an example of a therapist pursuing throughout the treatment the discussion of issues that threaten the viability of the therapy.

Suicidality

For most clinicians the greatest challenge borderline patients present to the therapy is in the form of self-destructive or suicidal threats or actions. This situation is experienced as especially difficult because the therapist is faced with deciding if the therapy is viable just when the patient may appear at greatest risk and in greatest need of help. In addition to clinical considerations, medicolegal concerns add to the complexity of the situation and compound the challenge to the therapist to maintain neutrality and clear thinking. A "medical model" approach to issues of responsibility in the treatment would argue that treaters who accept an impaired person into their care should do whatever they can to help or save that person. Such a position ignores the nature of borderline personality disorder since borderline patients may put themselves at risk precisely to provoke their therapists to become more involved in their lives by extending themselves beyond the frame of the therapy in terms of both time and emotional involvement.

Thus, an informed point of view with regard to the responsibility of therapists in the exploratory treatment of borderline patients would take into account the need both for therapists to define their role as one of reflection rather than action, and for the treatment arrangements not to feed into a cycle in which the therapists' response to acting-out behaviors provides gratifications that reward those behaviors and support their escalation. It is by no means the case that therapists following our recommendations would be shirking their legal and ethical responsibilities. The treatment we describe has built-in safeguards in the form of 1) advance planning as to how both therapist and patient will respond to the patient's suicidal impulses; 2) emphasis on the quality of communication between patient and therapist; and 3) the high priority placed on addressing suicidality when it is an issue.

In dealing with the patient's suicidality, it is essential for the therapist to clarify two points. The first is whether the suicidal or self-destructive ideation is a function of the patient's ongoing borderline personality organization or a symptom of an episode of affective illness. If the latter is the case—if the patient is experiencing a major depression—the work of the exploratory therapy is suspended and appropriate measures are taken to deal with the episode of illness. These measures might include referring the patient for a psychopharmacological consultation (even if the therapist is a psychiatrist, it is recommended that medications be prescribed by someone else) or having the patient admitted to a hospital.

If the therapist is satisfied that the self-destructive ideation is a function of the patient's borderline dynamics, the second point to clarify is whether the patient can benefit at this point from continuing in the therapeutic effort to increase understanding or if the patient requires concrete, practical, active intervention. If the latter is the case, the help needed is beyond the frame of the therapy. This distinction is often not clear in the minds of many patients and, indeed, of many therapists. If the therapy is viewed as a general and nonspecific commitment to do whatever possible to help a patient with emotional and behavioral difficulties—a view fostered both by the medical model of psychiatry and by a nonspecific, undifferentiated approach to psychotherapy—then it is not an exploratory therapy.

Insofar as exploratory therapy includes the goal of increasing the patient's mastery of her life, it discourages techniques that put the responsibility for decisions and actions in the hands of the therapist. If the patient does need help in organizing her life in a practical way, two options are available. One is for the patient to seek the help of a case manager/counselor at that point and consider exploratory therapy later on. The other is to work in psychotherapy and with a case manager in tandem. The evaluating therapist can help the patient with this decision.

The latter arrangement would involve referring the patient to a social worker with whom the therapist has a good working relationship for the practical help she needs. Whatever the arrangement, it is inadvisable for a therapist to begin exploratory work with a patient who has no external structure—school, volunteer work, or job—in her life. The therapist can point out to a patient who seeks treatment in these circumstances that therapy is not a substitute for involvement in the world and recommend that she set up some form of structured activity.

In formulating the treatment of a patient whose history includes self-destructive actions that have disrupted past therapies, the therapist should make clear to the patient how self-destructive actions will be viewed and treated in the context of the therapy under discussion. What follows is an example of such a discussion. The main guidelines of the discussion are summarized in figure 4.1.

In the past your suicide attempts and gestures became the focus of your interactions with your therapists. In your most recent therapy, you would call Dr. Black at night saying you felt suicidal, or you would say that you could not leave his office at the end of a session because you felt like killing yourself. He would extend sessions or call the crisis team for you or take you to the emergency room. One might say that he became your around-the-clock emergency service. This approach is one option to try to help you deal with your self-destructiveness. A serious disadvantage of this approach, however, is that, as happened in your treatment with Dr. Black, the treatment tends to dwell so much on your actions that it is difficult to work on understanding what

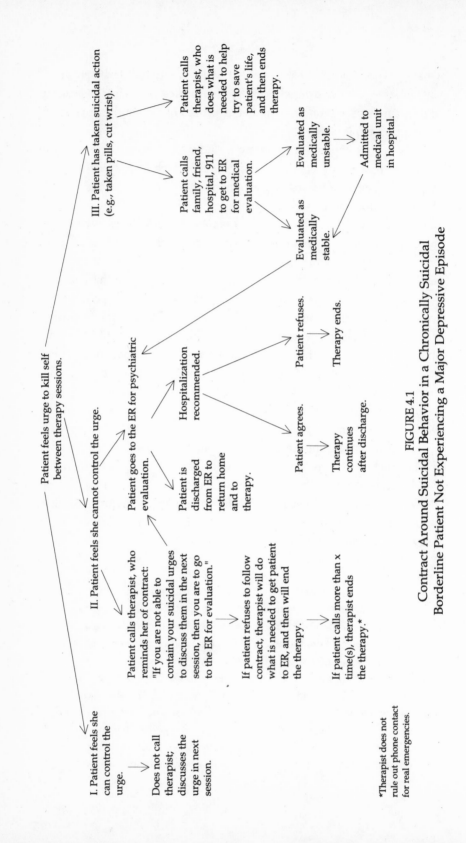

FIGURE 4.1

Contract Around Suicidal Behavior in a Chronically Suicidal
Borderline Patient Not Experiencing a Major Depressive Episode

deeper feelings underlie and motivate your actions. My evaluation leads me to believe that the kind of therapy with the most potential for helping you move beyond the problems you describe is one based on trying to understand the conflicts currently outside of your awareness. These are the feelings that lead to your repeatedly breaking off relationships, losing jobs, feeling angry, getting desperate, making suicide attempts, and so on.

While you may say you agree with this, but see no conflict between this point of view and your behavior in therapy with Dr. Black, I see it differently. If we engage in a therapy aimed at exploring your inner feelings and conflicts, any active involvement on my part in your life would hurt my ability to observe, reflect on, and try to understand what underlies your actions. I cannot get caught up in the action of your life and carry out exploratory therapy with you at the same time. *(The therapist is describing in layman's terms the need to observe therapeutic neutrality.)*

Therefore, if you are interested, I would like to describe to you the approach to your suicidal feelings required by this kind of therapy. When you feel suicidal, it will be your responsibility to evaluate your ability to control and contain that feeling. If you feel you can contain it, you can then discuss it in the next session. If you cannot contain the feeling, it will be up to you to take whatever steps are necessary to safeguard your life. This could include calling family or friends, the county crisis team, or the police. It might be a question of your going directly to a hospital emergency room or admitting office for an evaluation. Whoever is evaluating you may try to contact me for information, but it will be up to them—not me—to make the final decision.

In such a case, I would expect you to accept fully the recommendation coming out of the evaluation. If admission were recommended and you refused it, I would not be able to continue therapy with you since you would be placing yourself in a situation judged to be dangerous. Our therapy requires that we feel safe to explore whatever is on your mind. This would not be the case if we both knew that you had rejected a recommendation to go into the hospital.

Once in the hospital you would be in the care of the hospital team, and I would not have an active role in your treatment until it was time to plan for your discharge. At that time I would discuss with you and your inpatient therapist the indications regarding our resuming therapy. That would be an important moment for reflection on both of our parts—for you to reflect again on the kind of therapy that would be most helpful for you, and for me to review our treatment arrangements to see if any changes would be necessary.

What I've described so far assumes that you got yourself to an emergency room before taking any self-destructive action. The situation may arise where you have acted in a suicidal way before contacting anyone else. This possibility is, of course, a reflection of the real risk that you could successfully take your life. As I have said before, your life is ultimately in your hands; while I can try to help you gain more mastery over your self-destructiveness, I cannot guarantee your safety—only you can do that. In the case where you have taken suicidal action, such as an overdose, and then decide to try to save your life, your responsibility would be to get to an emergency room for a medical evaluation and subsequent psychiatric evaluation. Once again, it is up to you to decide whether to call family, friends, the police, or the crisis team. If you were found to be medically unstable, you would be admitted to a medical unit before the question of your further psychiatric care was decided. If you refused this admission, I would end therapy with you rather than cooperate with your putting yourself in an unsafe situation, as in the case I just described, if you were to reject the recommendation for psychiatric admission.

Comment

Having described these expectations with regard to the patient's management of her suicidal impulses, the therapist would ask for the patient's reaction to these conditions of therapy. The therapist should keep the following two main points in mind:

1. Facile acceptance by the patient may correspond to a devaluing disregard for everything the therapist has said (a "you can say what you want, I'll just deal with this therapy my own way" attitude). Therefore, the therapist must inquire further about an apparently quick agreement ("I'd like to hear a little more about your understanding of what I've said and your reaction to it") while not dwelling on the need for such a detailed, point-by-point repetition and agreement by the patient that the contract setting becomes an obsessive, lifeless exercise rather than a meaningful dialogue (see chapter 6, the first case presented, for an example of this pitfall).

2. Any detail, however small, of the expectations described by the

therapist can become the field on which the patient's attitudes and resistance unfold. Beginning therapists often feel that the main issue here is the patient's agreement to the overall principle being discussed, in this case the idea that if the patient becomes suicidal she will seek help and evaluation through the community's resources. However, overlooking details at this point is unwise for two reasons: strong resistance, which otherwise might be unheeded, may become apparent around the discussion of a relatively minor detail; and not being specific about the patient's expected management of a threat to the treatment can lead to confusion at a later point which the patient may capitalize on to derail the treatment.

An example of the therapist's pursuit, during the contract-setting phase, of a patient's unwillingness to accept one detail of the proposed conditions concerning suicidality is discussed in the chapter on establishing the contract in *Psychodynamic Psychotherapy of Borderline Patients* (Kernberg et al., 1989). The patient objects to the expectation that if she feels she cannot contain her suicidal impulses, she should seek evaluation in a psychiatric emergency room. She says she will go to a medical emergency room, but not a psychiatric one. After stating that this disagreement might keep them from beginning therapy, the therapist asks the patient her reasons for objecting to a psychiatric emergency room. In this situation there are two important points: 1) the therapist must feel comfortable with the possibility that the patient may reject the conditions of treatment, making this therapy impossible. For this reason therapists must be sure that they are describing the minimum conditions necessary to allow treatment to take place; and 2) the pursuit of the patient's objection may lead to valuable data, such as denial of the psychiatric nature of her difficulties, contempt for psychiatrists, or a wish to turn to internists if she cannot get from psychiatrists the overt sympathy and caretaking she wishes for.

Returning to our general example, after having discussed the patient's reaction to the conditions described thus far with regard to the threat that the patient's self-destructive urges pose to the treatment, the therapist goes on to explain what would happen if she deviated from the expected management of suicidal impulses:

> If you call me between sessions with questions about your self-destructiveness, I will suggest you discuss these feelings in our next session.

If you say you cannot wait until then, I will remind you that it is your responsibility to contact a hospital emergency room or admitting office. If you say you will not do that and insist on involving me in the situation, I will do everything I can at that time to try to help you get the crisis intervention you need, and then I will consider the therapy ended since you will have involved me in your life and self-destructive actions beyond the frame of the therapy. Similarly, if you call me to announce that you are about to take or have taken suicidal action, such as an overdose, and have not taken the responsibility to get to a hospital, I will do everything I can on that occasion to help try to save your life, and then will consider the therapy ended.

Comment

Patients may accuse therapists at this point of negligence with regard to their status as health professionals: "So, you're not really offering to help me; you're setting up a situation where I pay you to take care of me and your main concern is that I won't bother you." Clarification of the nature of exploratory therapy and of the need to frame the therapy so that it stands a chance of surviving where other therapies have failed may have to be repeated a number of times for the patient to understand that the conditions being presented are requirements of the treatment, not the personal wishes of the therapist.

> I'd like to remind you that the plan I'm proposing for therapy is based on what I know of you from our evaluation sessions, your history, and the history of your prior therapies. But before we get to that, I would also like to explain again that the type of treatment I'm recommending is a therapy focusing on the exploration of your inner feelings and conflicts. Your idea that you would be paying me to "take care of you" suggests you have a different kind of treatment in mind—something like case management with a counselor who would help you make decisions and get through your life on a day-to-day basis because you both agreed that you were not able to function independently.
>
> While that kind of treatment is an option for you, I have not recommended it since you have had that kind of help for so long without experiencing any appreciable long-term improvement in your ability to cope with life and get any satisfaction from it. In fact, one of the reasons you gave for seeking out an exploratory form of therapy

was that you had repeatedly disrupted your relations with a number of case managers because of recurrent angry arguments in which you accused them of intentionally working against you.

You still have the option of trying to work with a case manager again, and we can discuss that further. However, the immediate issue with regard to the subject of case management is why you have not been able to use that kind of help to make changes in your behavior patterns. If you are convinced that what you need now is further case management, or any other form of treatment different from the one I am recommending for you, it would be important for you to make that clear right now so that we do not take up more time discussing a treatment you are not interested in.

If you would like to hear more about this treatment, I can respond to your concern that the conditions of the therapy would have the purpose of serving my interests at the expense of yours. *(Patient expresses interest in hearing more.)* As I said, these conditions are based on what we know of you and your history. We know that in your prior therapy you called Dr. Black so often between sessions to report suicidal impulses that he could no longer distinguish between a situation of true seriousness and one of "crying wolf." Under these circumstances he did not feel that it was safe for him to continue to treat you. He also reported that it was hard for him to remain attentive and objective while listening to you in sessions because your late night calls often left him exhausted.

All therapists are human, and I am no exception. In that sense there is some truth to what you say about my defining these conditions to "keep you from bothering me." Insofar as your behavior between sessions with Dr. Black bothered him to the point that he could no longer work with you, I am proposing conditions to protect the treatment. These conditions include protecting my ability to keep working in a therapeutic way in relation to you.

Homicidality

The issue of homicidality is addressed both as it concerns people outside of the therapy and also as it concerns the therapist. The therapist may be involved directly, as a potential target of violence, or indirectly through the legal complications that may stem from having to make judgments about when to notify a third party of risk. If the issue of potential homicidality comes up in the evaluation and contract setting, the therapist first explains the legal obligation to inform an outside party who may be at risk. The therapist goes on to discuss with the patient how such an eventuality would be detrimental to the therapy as well as to the rest of the patient's life: It would distract them both from their mutual endeavor of understanding. Once again the underlying principle is that anything that takes away from the therapist's ability to maintain a neutral, comfortable, and safe position while trying to observe and understand the workings of the patient's mind may render the therapy ineffective.

With regard to the therapist's safety, it is evident that therapists cannot maintain a neutral observing stance vis-à-vis a patient who is actively threatening them. These threats would include threats to body, reputation, family, or property and would also include threats communicated by or involving others, such as a family member or boyfriend. Therapists' stated concern for themselves may be useful for patients who often suffer profound problems in self-esteem and for whom an identification with the therapist may be part of the therapeutic process.

It is important here to distinguish between a patient who may be elaborating a fantasy about the therapist—a perfectly valid use of therapy—and one who is expressing direct homicidal ideation. The therapist might say:

> While I can understand that in the course of therapy you might feel angry at me and may discuss that anger in sessions in vivid language and images, what you are saying right now sounds different in quality. I want to make it clear that our work would become impossible if you made any attempt to follow through on this idea that if you don't get better soon you would feel justified in having your boyfriend come to "rough me up."
>
> While this therapy is based on your reporting freely whatever comes into your mind, if it appears to me that what you are saying indicates that you cannot sufficiently control your impulses to carry out hostile, aggressive acts toward me, I will have to take what steps I can to ensure my safety. Most likely I would ask you to go to an emergency room or hospital admitting office for evaluation. If you refused to go along with that recommendation, or if the threat seemed too immediate to allow for that, I would be forced to call the clinic security guards or the police. If this happened, we could discuss the

situation later in a setting where we both felt safe—for example, in a hospital room with a guard present—in order to explore whether or not to continue therapy. However, in most such cases the therapy could not go on.

Problems Involving Attendance
or Active Participation

Having addressed threats to the patient's and therapist's lives and safety in an effort to keep them both available for treatment, the next most serious threat to the treatment is any pattern of overt or covert nonparticipation. The classic example is the patient who failed to attend sessions regularly during a prior therapy or who misses several sessions during the evaluation period. The problem may appear self-evident—therapy cannot happen if the two parties are not present—but it is not necessarily an easy one for the therapist to address. Appeals are often made by the patient based on the impossibility of regular attendance:

> In my line of work you never know when the boss is going to spring an emergency job on you. . . . I have to rely on the baby sitter and you never know when she's going to get there. . . . My husband drives me here and he doesn't understand the importance of being on time. . . . My colitis/migraines/PMS acts up and I just can't leave the house.

The therapist often begins to feel that the basic requirements of therapy, such as attending sessions, are harsh, rigid, or even sadistic demands. When this happens, the therapist should reflect on what is developing in the transference and countertransference. On the most real level, while the effort to get to sessions may indeed be considerable, one should not forget that for a patient whose life may be threatened by her illness, treatment is a high priority.

The best strategy at such a moment is to keep in mind two dynamic principles. The first is resistance. Whatever the reality of the difficulty in attending regularly, it may also be in the service of resistance. The task of honestly examining one's inner world is inevitably daunting—especially for patients whose internal world is characterized by intense, unintegrated affects—and while it is appropriate to empathize with the difficulty of that task, one must always be alert to the risk of colluding with resistance.

The second principle is countertransference. Any reaction by the therapist to the patient's appeal—for example, to become concerned that an expectation may be harsh and sadistic—should be viewed as relevant to understanding the patient's inner world. While it would be premature for therapists to change the focus to interpretation at this point, they should enter this data into their emerging formulation, reminding themselves:

> I'm beginning to feel punitive and sadistic toward this patient. This must relate to one of the patient's patterns of object relations. I should watch for the appearance of this affect in this relationship dyad and also be aware that, because the poles of the dyad may shift, I can expect to be on the receiving end of some punitive and sadistic behavior from her at some later point.

The countertransference could also have another, and perhaps more subtle, role here if the therapist were actually to agree that this patient should not be expected to attend sessions regularly. While this response may appear to be understanding and sympathetic on the surface, it may, in fact, represent the therapist's having accepted the projected role of sadist since adopting this position would mean participating in the patient's attempt to undo the very activity that may be her best hope for survival.

The simple fact that must be communicated to the patient at this point is that the treatment cannot happen if she is not there. In the case of a patient who has a history of irregular attendance in a prior therapy, the therapist might say:

> Since you've missed two of the five sessions we've scheduled so far and since your attendance at your prior therapy was very irregular, we need to address the possibility that you will not attend sessions here regularly—a situation that would keep us from working together to understand your problems. The treatment needs you to be here, and so at this point I would like to know if you agree that you must come to every scheduled session and are willing to make a commitment to do so. If you disagree with this expectation, we should discuss it now.

It may turn out that you do not agree with, or do not feel able to go along with, what this treatment requires. If that is the case, it is better to know that now rather than to embark on the treatment under circumstances that would eventually undermine it.

Another possibility is that you might agree to attend regularly now but would later begin to repeat the pattern of missing many sessions. You should know that if this becomes the case we will have to review the situation to see if the therapy can go on. Since the therapy cannot take place without you here, it would make more sense to end the treatment than to go on as though you were in treatment when the reality was otherwise.

Comment

If the patient then readily agrees to this requirement of treatment, the therapist needs to review the patient's previous behaviors to determine the extent to which the patient has thought about them herself. ("Your car kept breaking down and you refused to go by bus so you missed a lot of sessions with your previous therapist. What's changed?")

Therapists in training often ask: "How many sessions can a patient miss before I end the treatment with her?" This way of phrasing the question suggests that two key concepts have not yet been appreciated. First, it is not the therapist who ends the treatment; it is the patient who, through her undermining actions, may make the treatment impossible and thereby end it. The therapist merely points out that this is happening. Second, the idea that there is an absolute number of missed sessions that determines when the treatment is rendered ineffective suggests that the therapist is abdicating making a clinical judgment in favor of an objective and procrustean rule that can be applied to every patient in every therapy. While such a position might seem easier to therapists, it is their responsibility to decide when missing sessions constitutes a pattern or trend that undermines the therapy. To choose a fixed number of missed sessions in advance may play into the patient's projection onto the therapist of a rigid and arbitrary other who imposes rules to which the patient must submit.

This strategy may also lead to a game of "chicken" in which the patient gradually approaches the magic number of sessions, usually at a time of apparently compelling crisis, as though to dare the therapist to carry out the "threat of" ending the treatment. While it is possible to interpret this development if it occurs, a more therapeutic frame is provided by an initial understanding that if missing sessions becomes an issue in the treatment, the problem will have to be discussed in terms of whether it is rendering the therapy impossible. This approach communicates the importance of the issue and leaves therapists room to explore it adequately without painting themselves into a corner.

Although it may seem obvious that treatment cannot take place without the patient present, this simple reality should be stated to a borderline patient with a history of missing sessions. One variant of the primitive defense of omnipotent control is for the patient to imagine that someone else can take care of her, even though that person does not have the means to act effectively in any real way.

A corollary of the attendance requirement is the need to be psychologically available in sessions. If there is any indication that the patient may come to sessions under the influence of alcohol or drugs, the therapist must explain that by making any effective work impossible, this behavior would lead to the end of that particular session and, if it became a pattern, to the end of the therapy (see chapter 6, pp. 146–48, for a discussion of this issue in the context of the second case presented).

"Nonlethal" Self-destructiveness

The outline discussed earlier regarding the therapist's position vis-à-vis suicidal behavior is relatively straightforward. However, patients often present with behaviors that are self-destructive without being lethal, such as superficial cutting or "mini" overdoses. Therapists are often uncertain how to consider these behaviors. From a dynamic point of view are they the same as suicidal behaviors? From a practical point of view should the same conditions of therapy hold for these behaviors as for behaviors with a clearly lethal potential? A typical reaction from a therapist struggling with developing an appropriate contract is: "I can understand the need for the patient to go to an emergency room if she is at risk of killing herself, but is that necessary if the patient is dealing with an urge to inflict a superficial cut?"

It is helpful in a situation like this to remember the principal rationale of contract setting: The purpose of the contract is to protect the therapy and allow it to take place. To put the question in terms of whether to apply the same contract conditions to issues of bodily integrity as to issues of potential lethality suggests that the purpose of the contract is to protect the patient's life. Although the contract is to protect the therapy, by implication it follows that this helps the patient take responsibility for her life. Yet it would be unrealistic, grandiose, and unsafe to think that the treatment—however careful the contract—can guarantee the patient's safety; only the patient can do that. Therefore, the main question for therapists to ask themselves is: "What will the impact of the 'nonlethal' self-destructive behaviors be on the work of the therapy?"

To answer that question the therapist must once again consider the patient's history and presentation. It is not enough to know the diagnosis and to try to apply a "standard" contract to all borderline patients. Exploratory therapy is based on the principle of allowing the patient to tell, to discover, and to examine her own story. A diagnosis helps the therapist begin to conceptualize the case of a new patient and to set up an adequate frame for the treatment. It is important to keep in mind, however, that the frame is not the picture; it allows the picture to emerge.

The process of therapy will be an ongoing refinement of ways to understand the patient. Consequently, conditions of treatment may have to be introduced or revised if issues arise that were not presented or were not clear during the contract-setting phase. It is unreasonable to expect that a therapist will always discern in advance all the possible threats that a particular patient will introduce into the treatment. It is also possible that a patient may develop new undermining behaviors. Therefore, the therapist should continue to scan for such developments and be prepared to introduce new parameters as needed at any point in the treatment. With regard to self-mutilating actions, the therapist does not know at this point if the patient cuts herself because it is a learned behavior for coping with anger, a derivative of undifferentiated libidinal and aggressive drives, a repetition of a history of physical abuse, an attempt to influence or make the therapist squirm, or some combination of all of these.

Returning to the question of contracting with regard to nonlethal, self-destructive behaviors, the main consideration is the degree to

107

which these behaviors are likely to undermine the exploratory therapy. Some cases are relatively straightforward. A young woman's prior therapy of three years was characterized by her repeatedly cutting and burning herself to the extent that her therapist's role was largely confined to monitoring the extent of these behaviors and evaluating her condition to determine if it was necessary for her to seek medical treatment or be admitted to a hospital. In this case the evaluating therapist's position was:

> Your prior therapy was rendered ineffective by your cutting and burning yourself when these acts became the focus of the work and made it impossible to use the sessions to explore your feelings and conflicts. You led your therapist on an endless chase after your self-destructive actions. It may even have been the case, as you have suggested, that your therapist was inhibited from actively pursuing the work of exploration for fear that if he said the wrong thing, you would go home and hurt yourself.
>
> I would like to emphasize that as your therapist I am interested in your actions, or symptoms, only to the extent that looking at them will help us understand more about you and *get beyond them*. If you continue to engage in self-destructive behaviors while in therapy, I would wonder with you if this was your way of communicating that you are not interested in this type of exploration and are, in fact, electing to end the treatment. If so, case management would be more appropriate for you, since that type of treatment would focus on the level of these symptomatic actions and behaviors.
>
> Still, the very fact that you are here for an evaluation is a sign that part of you is interested in exploring your actions and getting beyond them. To avoid inhibiting the exploratory work here as happened before, we need to be free of the preoccupation that you might be inflicting tissue damage. Therefore, I recommend that you take some time to think about the kind of treatment you are interested in before signing on here.

Comment

The therapist communicates a number of important things through these comments. First, he expects that the patient will give up engaging in self-destructive behaviors and attempt to understand what lies behind them. Second, he presents a model for reflecting on action rather than acting impulsively ("I would wonder . . ."). Third, the therapist makes clear it would not be his action, but hers, that ended the therapy; he does not say: "If you cut yourself or burn yourself, I will end the therapy." That position, while arguable, runs the risk of the therapist's reflecting back to the patient harsh and rigid superego precursors that would be better analyzed than acted out in the countertransference.

There are, nonetheless, instances in which the therapist might set a more specific contingency to self-destructive behaviors than in the previous example. One case is that of a patient with a history of repeated hospitalizations in which she continued to cut herself. Finally, this patient showed that she had control over her behavior when she was told in one hospital that if she cut herself there, she would be transferred to a state hospital. During the evaluation for outpatient therapy at the time of discharge, the therapist asked why the patient had stopped cutting herself in the hospital. The patient replied without hesitation that it was the understanding that if she did so, she would be transferred. The therapist asked if the patient thought it would be helpful in controlling her self-destructive urges to have an analogous under-standing in the therapy. Since they both knew that her previous cutting had interrupted outpatient therapy on many occasions, but that she was capable of controlling her urges to cut herself, they would understand that any cutting from this point on was a sign that the patient was electing to end the therapy. The patient, while acknowledging some reluctance to do so, agreed that this understanding would benefit the therapy. In a case like this the therapist may worry that the patient might agree to the understanding but then withhold information about cutting. A therapist who has this concern could decide to institute a system of "body checks," in which the patient would meet periodically with a nurse who would examine her body for any evidence of new self-destructive behavior.

Another group of self-destructive behaviors found in this patient population are eating disorders. The therapist could relegate the practi-cal care and monitoring of the patient's weight and nutritional status to an internist. Alternatively, the therapist could set up a system of periodic weight checks, to be carried out by a nurse or dietitian. If the patient were to go below a predetermined weight, she would have to begin a prearranged weight-gaining protocol and the focus of her therapy would then be on the meaning of the weight loss since, as a threat to the treatment, it is high on the hierarchy of thematic priorities to be addressed in this form of treatment. If the patient's weight loss persisted and concerns about the patient's health made it impossible to concentrate on the exploratory work, the therapy might have to be suspended. For a patient with a history of bulimia nervosa, the therapist could consider having a nurse or internist monitor the patient's amylase level, potassium level, and the condition of her teeth.

Intrusions into the Therapist's Life

The issue of intrusions into the therapist's life is analogous to the issue of homicidal threats to the therapist, but it differs insofar as the harm threatened is more psychological than physical and the actions involved may on the surface appear less aggressive. Behaviors in question may include calling the therapist repeatedly at home, spying on the therapist and his or her family, or appearing in public places to meet the therapist.

Phone calls are the most common intrusion. Indeed, many therapists believe that accepting calls between sessions is an expected and acceptable part of the therapeutic arrangement. It is not clear, however, that this practice advances the work of exploratory therapy. The experience of the authors includes evaluating many patients whose previous therapists seemed almost saintly in their willingness to talk to the patient between sessions but whose treatments ended when the demands of the patient increased, the patience of the therapist was exhausted, or both. This brings us back to the cardinal rule that therapists should agree to work only within conditions they can realistically tolerate and, if possible, that limits should be thought through and defined before a situation arises rather than after. Different therapists may have different levels of tolerance; the essential point is for them to have a realistic idea of their own limits and of the conditions they can work within and to keep these in mind when framing the treatment.

A careful history-taking often reveals whether phone calling has been a problem in past therapies. If so, the contracting therapist should present a structure for dealing with that eventuality. Since phone calls, if contained, are less immediately harmful and distracting from the work of therapy than suicidal behaviors, the structure for dealing with phone calls provides for some intermediate contingencies not seen in the model presented earlier for dealing with suicide threats.

THERAPIST: While you say it was important for you that Dr. Jones accepted phone calls from you between sessions, it seems as though that practice contributed to the ending of the therapy. You were so enraged at him for not returning a call promptly enough that you took an overdose and wound up in the hospital. It was then that Dr. Jones recommended a change in therapist.

I would like to work out a policy around phone calls to minimize the risk of their interfering with our work in therapy. Aside from calls to communicate necessary information, such as having to cancel a session, I will accept phone calls from you only if the situation you are calling about is a true emergency. Since an emergency is an event that is both major and un-foreseen, it does not include either your self-destructive feelings, which are a chronic and longstanding condition, or regular upsetting events, such as one in a series of arguments with your boyfriend, your boss, or whomever. Emergencies would include such things as being in a serious accident, suddenly being fired from a job, testing HIV positive, being diagnosed with cancer, or learning of the death of someone close to you.

If you call me at my office or my home, let me know right away what the emergency is. If there is no emergency, I will refer you to the next session and will tell you that I will not answer any more calls from you for the next week. If you call after that, I will extend the period of not taking or answering calls to a month. If you do not refrain from calling at that point, I will extend the period to a year.

PATIENT: But how can you pretend to be my therapist if you won't even talk to me?

THERAPIST: I will be available to listen to you and talk to you during our scheduled sessions. The kind of therapy I'm recom-mending consists of persistent work toward understanding, not ad hoc trouble-shooting. And even if I felt it would be beneficial for you to have me available to you on an around-the-clock basis, it would not be realistic for me to offer that kind of arrangement. You are aware of the resources in this community and can use them if need be.*

Comment

Since this structure for dealing with inappropriate phone calls sets up the contingency of not accepting calls at all for a defined period, it would only be when a patient ignored the contingencies that the therapist might have to question if the therapy could continue. To avoid that eventuality, it is of course important to elicit the patient's reaction when explaining the structure that will apply to phone calls. Some readers may find this set of contingencies regarding phone calls to be arbitrary and extreme. However, in those cases where a patient's calls to the therapist's home disrupt family and home life, nothing short of this arrangement is adequate to contain the behavior and rechannel the patient's communications to the therapist into the framework of the sessions where work can be done.

More aggressive forms of intruding into the therapist's life, such as spying, do not allow for as much flexibility as the structure around phone calls. Since spying—which often represents the behavioral manifestation of pervasive paranoid and hostile beliefs—is never justified and suggests a serious inability to contain transferential feelings within the frame of the therapy, the therapist should make a clear statement that any instance of it would call for an immediate review of the viability of the treatment.

Efforts to Involve the Therapist in the Patient's Life

This category of threat to the treatment has already been addressed to some degree in the discussion of suicidal and self-destructive threats,

*Of course part of the evaluation of the patient is an assessment of the need for structure and practical assistance in the patient's life. Recommendations may range from telling a patient who is unemployed but capable of work that it is important for her to take on the responsibility and structure of a job to telling a recently hospitalized patient that she would benefit from the transitional structure of a day program, volunteer job, and/or the temporary help of a case manager to assist with practical living problems.

insofar as those behaviors include an element of trying to draw therapists out of their role and into "real life" interactions with their patient.
The suicidal and self-destructive examples were discussed in separate
sections of this chapter, both because they are common in borderline
patients and because they often elicit a special level of anxiety in
therapists. In examining a patient's history and behavior, however, one
may find other ways in which she attempts to involve therapists. Although more benign on the surface, these may prove to be equally
destructive to the therapy.

One example of this situation is the patient who, in addition to
therapy, is in a day hospital or other program and either tells the
program or lets the staff there assume that the therapist is the coordina-
tor of all aspects of her treatment. The day program may then call the
therapist whenever the patient is acting out to ask the therapist what to
do or may report to the therapist that they will stop treating the patient
if her behavior does not improve. While a program has every right to
determine its parameters of treatment, as does a therapist, the program's
calling the therapist, rather than focusing on confronting the patient,
implies that the therapist, and not the patient, is responsible for the
patient's actions. This line of communication exerts pressure on the
therapist to deviate from a position of neutrality. The exploratory
therapist's role is to explore with the patient the meaning of her jeopard-
izing her treatment at the day program. Yet, it may be difficult to
maintain neutrality when other professionals are pressuring the therapist
to take an active role in the patient's life outside the sessions.

The situation may be further complicated if the therapist had
initially made attending a day program a prerequisite for therapy. Such
a prerequisite would most often be made in the case of a patient starting
therapy upon being discharged from an inpatient unit. The therapist
would have explained that therapy would have little chance of succeeding without additional structure during the rest of the week. This way
of formulating the situation makes it the responsibility of the patient to
arrange for a day program if she wants to pursue the therapy, and
further reinforces the principle that therapy exists to observe life, not
manage it. Very often, however, the patient's statement in applying for
day treatment ("My therapist said I should be in this program") is
understood by the program administrator to mean that the therapist is
responsible for the patient. In other words, the therapist's effort to

explain to the patient what conditions (that is, the day program) would increase the patient's likelihood of being able to use exploratory therapy is understood as the therapist's offering to assume responsibility for coordinating all aspects of the patient's care. In the abstract it may seem as if we are drawing a fine line when we say that the therapist *consults* with the patient about what is necessary (a day program, a job, or the like) in order to give exploratory therapy a chance to happen but that the therapist *is not in charge* of the patient's taking on such activities. In actual treatment situations, however, the implications are very significant. It is the therapist's responsibility to determine what kind of therapy is indicated, to decide what conditions would make the treatment possible, and to determine if those conditions are being met adequately for the treatment to proceed.

To guard against the misunderstanding that the therapist is responsible for the patient's treatment beyond the therapy and the subsequent risk of being called on to intervene if the patient's behavior is threatening her tenure at the day program, it is advisable for therapists to explain clearly not only to the patient but also to the administrator of the day program that they are offering the patient an exploratory therapy that does not include case management. If the patient is judged to be unable to coordinate the different aspects of her treatment and her life, the therapist can refer her to a skilled case manager or social worker to assume that function.

Having explained to the patient the basis for recommending a day program, the therapist can go on to predict the risk that the patient may use the day program as a way to draw the therapist out of the neutral role:

> I want to clarify two things about my recommendation regarding day hospital treatment. First, it is your responsibility to arrange for that part of your treatment and to do whatever it takes to maintain yourself in that program for as long as the director of the program recommends. If, for whatever reason, you drop out of the program or are asked to leave, I would at that time review the possibility of our continuing this therapy under that circumstance.
>
> The second point is that I am recommending the day program as indicated from the point of view of your therapy; my recommendation does not mean that I have any authority over that part of your

treatment or any responsibility to that part of your treatment. Even in making this recommendation, I recognize that there are ways you could use the day program to attempt to distract us from our exploration in therapy. One form of distraction would be to stir up the concern of the staff at the day program until they called on me to get involved in dealing with a problem you were having there. If this became the case, I would remind them that my role is limited to helping you investigate the meaning of your actions and feelings. A second way you might engage the day program to distract us would be to create the feeling that there was a conflict between our work and your work there. For instance, you might report to them that I was denying you adequate time to deal with the feelings that come up in therapy and that it was my unwillingness to extend sessions that led to your agitated behavior in the program. If this situation arose, the staff at the program might even question the value of your continuing in therapy. In this circumstance I would ask you to reflect on what it meant that you were arousing animosity between different elements of your treatment and provoking others to take a position against your therapy.

If the staff of your day program asked to speak with me, I would do so providing I had your consent. In any communication with them I would remind them of the specific role I have in your treatment, discuss any hypothesis I might have about the meaning of your behavior, and decline to accept any responsibility for you beyond that of the work of exploratory therapy.

Comment

This example describes only one of many possible ways a patient might try to engage the therapist beyond the limits of therapy. Similar efforts could be made to involve the therapist in family or marital problems, issues of custody, school difficulties, legal entanglements, and so on. The basic rule of contracting relevant here is to try to anticipate any forseeable way the patient may attempt to involve the therapist in her life and to explain in advance the position that would then be required of the therapist by this form of therapy. Since it is rarely possible to predict all eventualities, it is also helpful to make a general statement along these lines:

As my description of the therapy suggests, if you were to create situations that involved me in your life in some active way, I would take the position of examining why you were doing so. If it were necessary for me at any point to become involved in your life outside of therapy, I would limit that involvement to a minimum and resume our work of exploration as quickly as possible. Our first priority would then be to examine the meaning and impact of your drawing me into your life and to address the question of whether working together in exploratory therapy remained possible.

Problems Created Outside Sessions

The preceding sections of this chapter have dealt with ways the patient's actions threaten the frame of the therapy directly through her behavior toward the sessions or the therapist. Patients can also threaten the viability of the therapy by indirect actions. Typical examples of this behavior might be creating a situation in which the patient cannot pay the fee (losing a job, discontinuing insurance, alienating parents who help fund the therapy, and so on) or one in which it is impossible for the patient to attend sessions at regular times (taking a job with an unpredictable schedule.)

If her history suggests that a patient is likely to create any such complicating factors, therapists must address these in much the same way that they would address any of the challenges to treatment discussed earlier. These situations are different only in the degree that 1) their superficially indirect connection to the therapy may make it initially more difficult for the therapists to see the pattern of undermining the treatment; and 2) their indirect relation to the therapy may be used in the service of the patient's denial of her responsibility for the potential threat to the treatment. An example of a therapist's discussion of such a threat is as follows:

Each of the times you were in therapy before, you lost your job and had to stop therapy for lack of funds. You said how unreasonable you felt each of your bosses was, and I know you considered it their fault rather than yours that you lost those jobs. I am not in a position to comment on their contribution to those situations; however, loss of a job has had a clear role in ending your therapy three times. If you decide to enter into therapy with me, we could examine what connections there might be between your being in therapy and your losing those jobs. The pattern of job losses suggests, however, that this therapy might soon be in danger as well. The most helpful message I can offer you now is that for reasons we do not yet understand, you may have contributed to forcing an end to your prior therapies. It will take time to understand what the underlying reasons were. In the meantime, you may be at risk for repeating this pattern. I can only point out to you the likelihood of this and recommend that you pay attention to any such developments. As you know from your prior experiences, if you do find yourself without the means to pay for therapy, you will effectively be ending the possibility of our working together.

Summary

The discussions in this chapter have delineated ways in which a borderline patient may present with certain predictable and recognizable threats to the work of exploratory psychotherapy. We have attempted to demonstrate ways of framing the treatment that will decrease, although not eliminate, the threat of sabotage. There is no question that patients may yet find ways to threaten the treatment, ways that have not been included in this discussion. In such cases we encourage therapists to keep in mind the central principle of defining conditions of treatment that protect their ability to think clearly in the context of the therapy. If therapists evaluating a patient perceive a new kind of threat to the treatment which they have not had the opportunity to think through fully and logically, they should feel free to tell the patient that they will need more time to reflect on this development and that they will have more to say about it in the next session. Therapists who feel obliged to come up immediately with an appropriate and definitive response to every situation the patient brings up are probably acting under the influence of the idealizing transference that calls on them to assume an impossible position of omnipotence.

CHAPTER 6

The Collaborative Element: Two Problem Sessions

A TREATMENT CONTRACT sets a tone for the therapy that is to follow. Ideally, the contract phase is characterized above all by the mutual respect of the prospective therapist and patient for each other's position without compromising what is required for psychotherapy to take place. Inadequate attention to the requirements of the therapy often leads to a diluted semblance of therapy, or, worse, the degeneration of therapy into the mutual enactment of a primitive drama. To avoid these pitfalls the therapist-to-be must be open to the patient's concerns and desires while never compromising on those issues deemed essential to the conduct of the treatment. Therapists need to be clear within themselves as to which are the necessary treatment conditions, why they are crucial, and how it might be difficult for the patient either to accept or to carry them out. In addition, therapists must articulate all this to their patients.

If the contract-setting experience is a collaborative one in which the patient feels she has been understood and taken seriously (without the therapist necessarily being in total agreement with her), then she will carry that experience over into the treatment that is to follow. By the same token, should the patient experience the therapist as being either wishy-washy about principles initially described as essential, or as rigidly defending a position to be sure of maintaining control, then that will have negative consequences for the treatment.

In this chapter we present two contract-setting experiences that superficially appear quite different. What they have in common is the therapist's failure to present the contract setting as a collaborative process. Both therapists ignore the patient's input into the process—the first by rigidly adhering to her own agenda, the second by avoiding taking up with the patient any of his concerns about the agreement. In both instances, dynamic interaction has been replaced by ritual.

Case Study #1

In the first session to be discussed, the therapist is rigorous in her adherence to the letter of the law of contract setting, but fails to capture any of its spirit. She obsessively articulates rules and regulations, while conveying this information in a manner that does not show any appreciation of the patient's contribution and, as a result, encourages her opposition.

Some readers of this example have questioned its veracity, suggesting it might have been exaggerated in a way that makes it painful to read. Yet, the example is taken directly from a clinical session. The fact that it may seem unrealistically extreme is evidence of the power of the forces that come into play in the interaction between patient and therapist—particularly, in this case, the power of the countertransference. The authors acknowledge that the example does not make for the best prose or easiest reading but felt that it should be included in its entirety for didactic purposes, precisely because it conveys some sense of the extreme discomfort that many therapists report in their efforts to take on the challenge of borderline patients.

> THERAPIST: Today we're going to be talking about how we're going to be carrying out our work. Basically what we're going to be talking about is the framework of the treatment, how things are going to be set up, what your responsibilities are, and what are my responsibilities. Also, based on your history, we'll

discuss the possible difficulties that might arise should we agree to begin the treatment. . . .

PATIENT: *(Interrupting)* OK.

THERAPIST: . . . to anticipate those things and to hopefully prevent them from happening and to consider what we'll do if they do happen.

PATIENT: Uh hm.

THERAPIST: First, why don't we start with your responsibilities? We will be meeting twice a week . . .

PATIENT: Uh hm.

THERAPIST: . . . for forty-five minutes. We'll be meeting on Mondays and Thursdays, from 9:30 to 10:15. These sessions will begin on time and they will end on time. It's important for you to be there on time. It's important that you stay to the end of the sessions. If, for whatever reason, things get difficult, you must not leave in the middle of the session.

Comment

The therapist speaks only of the requirements, not of the people who are to be the participants. She says that it is the "sessions" that will begin and end on time rather than, "We will begin and end . . ." She implies that "it's important for you to be there on time" because that's when the sessions begin, giving a sterile and autocratic cast to the experience. Alternatively, she might have said, "As you've made clear from the array of problems you mentioned during the history-taking phase, there are many issues that concern you, and therefore we will need all the time we have to work on your concerns," identifying the necessity for appearing on time because the patient has already defined an interest to which the therapist is responding.

This concept is basic to all work involved in establishing a contract, namely, that the "rules" of the contract derive neither capriciously nor from the therapist's private needs, but are logical extensions of what is required to carry out a program that addresses the patient's concerns. To underscore that point, it is useful, whenever possible, to show the patient the link between the particular issue under discussion and what the patient states is her desire. For example, "Since it is so important to you that you not be misunderstood, you must speak loudly enough for me to hear you." In doing so, the therapist begins in the contract phase to help the patient understand the continuity between her various thoughts and actions and what will be required of her if change is to occur. Also, identifying the contractual issues as necessary in pursuit of the patient's goals underscores the collaboration and emphasizes that therapists take their cue from their patients.

By relating contract interventions to the patient's statements, the therapist reinforces the value and necessity of the patient's contribution to her own treatment. When the therapist here adds, "If things, for whatever reason, get difficult, you must not leave in the middle of the session," she is speaking from a clearly authoritarian point of view and fails to communicate that she has any appreciation of why this might be difficult for the patient.

Wherever possible it is important to clarify that the components of the frame are essential, not because either the therapist or the patient necessarily wants them, but because without them the treatment cannot go on. Therefore, the accusation, "But doctor, if I could be doing this already (referring to whatever contract issue is under discussion), I wouldn't need you!" should be met first with an appreciation of the patient's concerns and, at the same time, with the statement that because these are the minimum conditions for conducting the treatment, the therapist is as helpless as the patient to change them.

Returning to the case example, one might alternatively say,

> From what you've already told me about yourself, it's clear that there will be many times when you will be tempted to leave the session. Though you have certainly helped me to see why this would be an appealing alternative for you, at the same time it must be clear to you that not only would you be continuing a pattern of behavior that you yourself decry, but more importantly, if you are not here, no work can go on between us.

Note that without making any promises, the therapist here is implicitly suggesting that reflection can lead, over time, to the patient's altering her behavior.

PATIENT: Uh hm.
THERAPIST: And it's important that you leave on time too.

PATIENT: Uh hm.

THERAPIST: It's important for you to be there or else we can't . . .

PATIENT: *(Interrupting)* Yeah.

THERAPIST: We can't do any work if you're not here. That makes sense?

PATIENT: Uh hm.

THERAPIST: Does that make sense to you?

PATIENT: Yeah. Monday is easy. I just seem to have a mental block for Thursday *(chuckling)*.

THERAPIST: There were a few times that you didn't come. You said you overslept.

Comment

When the therapist reminds the patient that there were "a few times that you didn't come; you said you overslept," she provides a context for why she is discussing the necessity for keeping appointments before the treatment can begin. In the chaotic and often disruptive world of the borderline patient, whose condition is often further compromised by paranoid belief systems, it helps to anchor one's interventions to observations of patient behaviors that both parties have shared. Thus, if the patient were to question or challenge the therapist's concern about a regular schedule, the therapist might then wonder with the patient why she is unable to link her past behavior (that is, oversleeping) with possible repetitions in the future.

You will soon hear the therapist commenting, "And I think we're going to want to take a look at what that's [oversleeping] all about." The importance here is the use of the future tense, "We're going to want," which means, paradoxically, that, in order for there to be a future outcome in which regular attendance becomes an issue that no longer requires examination, the patient must be present herself now. It is not enough to say, "We will look at this later and try to resolve it." What needs to be indicated is that this is a present problem that must be corrected if treatment is to take place.

PATIENT: Yeah, and it's twice this has happened and both times on a Thursday.

THERAPIST: We're going to want to take a look at what that's all about.

PATIENT: Usually I'm up at six every day. I don't understand.

THERAPIST: I think that's important to look at during our time together. The other thing that's going to be your responsibility is to make sure that you pay your bills on time. And . . .

PATIENT: *(Interrupting)* Medicaid takes care of that, right?

THERAPIST: Right, I know that you're on Medicaid.

PATIENT: Right.

THERAPIST: And they take care of the bills. Your responsibility will be that when you come, you show your card to the front desk.

PATIENT: Oh, I do?

THERAPIST: Isn't that what the procedure is?

PATIENT: No. No one told me that. I just come in.

THERAPIST: Basically what you'll do is come to the front desk with your Medicaid card. You'll show that to the front desk, and they'll run it through a machine that makes sure that your Medicaid card is updated. Is it up-to-date?

PATIENT: Right now it's invalid. I talked to the Social Security office and they said that they put the papers through, but the front office closed my case anyway. What they had to do is reopen it. Remember when you went and we talked to that lady at the front desk?

THERAPIST: Yes.

PATIENT: Ms. Smith. She wasn't able to get through, but I got through to someone who said he'd settle everything. I got a new card in the mail. It's invalid. I just found this out last week. He said he doesn't know why they closed it. It was just probably a mistake. The papers didn't go through in time.

THERAPIST: After this session would you go talk to Ms. Smith?

PATIENT: I don't have my card with me though.

THERAPIST: She'll probably have your number. Do you have time to talk to her today?

PATIENT: Not really 'cause I got to be at the dermatologist.

THERAPIST: I think it's pretty important that you need to have just five minutes to talk to her or at least give her a call.

Comment

The therapist's response to the patient's description of the problems she is having with her Medicaid card is to tell her what to do. "I think it's pretty important that you need to have just five minutes to talk to her or at least give her a call." In our introductory comments we mentioned that the way in which the contract setting is approached sets the stage for the treatment that is to follow. Wherever possible, the therapist's job is to help the patient identify the nature of the issue and then, together, define the extent to which the patient is able to deal with it on her own. Only when that limit has been reached should the therapist intervene, and even then by first attempting to discover whether the limitation is itself an expression of resistance.

This plan of operation is consistent with two core beliefs of psychodynamic psychotherapy: first, that interpretation should begin only at the point at which the patient is unable to figure things out on her own; and second, that analysis of the resistance takes precedence over anything else. A corollary of the contract-setting phase is the therapist's steadfast insistence, both through word and deed, that the patient bear a significant responsibility for the conduct of the work, which in this phase consists of determining whether a consensus can be reached on the conditions necessary for carrying out the treatment.

PATIENT: Yeah, I can call her. I can call her today from the Center at lunch time.

THERAPIST: It's important for you to keep your card updated.

PATIENT: Yeah. Oh, I know. I call every other day to make sure it gets done, but they said it's going to take at least a week. I called the guy yesterday, and he said he wants me to come in and show him my card. He wants to look at the card. Maybe there's something the matter with it. But I forgot my wallet in my friend's car Friday night, and she lives all the way out in Stony Brook. She was supposed to bring it to me yesterday. She never showed up, so I have to call her today to make sure she brings my card by Thursday, and we'll call that guy again today and tell him I don't have my card yet and I'll see if I can go on Thursday.

Comment

The patient makes a lengthy explanation which should raise suspicions in the therapist's mind that certain kinds of dilemma may emerge if the treatment takes place. The patient sees her world as full of problematic, interdependent factors that threaten to overwhelm and/or victimize her. The point here is not to make any such interpretation to the patient, but for the therapist to ask herself whether this information makes it necessary to ask the patient for further clarification of these issues as they might impinge on the treatment. For example, if the patient, in the course of the therapist's efforts to understand how she planned to pay her bill, were to react by saying that the therapist was making a mountain out of a molehill, the therapist could then refer to the patient's precarious sense of herself:

> As you explained to me when you were talking about your Medicaid card, you feel that to live your life in a responsible fashion takes an inordinate amount of effort and that, even with this effort, you may not be able to get the job done. One of the ways I know this is from all the things that went wrong about the Medicaid card. The administrator made things difficult for you, you forgot your wallet in your friend's car who lives very far away, she failed to show up, and you had to do all this work just to get another appointment. On that basis, can you see where I would think that being able to manage the details of your life might be very difficult for you and that this makes it all the more important to review how you will attend to the requirements of therapy?

The therapist is evaluating the patient's capacity to empathize with the rationale underlying the therapist's behavior. The more the patient is able to appreciate how the therapist's understanding of her creates the necessity for the particular frame of treatment, the more she and the therapist are working together.

What we are describing here is not the patient's wholesale endorsement of the therapist's position, but rather their arriving at a compact, an alliance between the therapist and that part of the patient that can observe herself. The more primitive the patient's ego organization, the more the therapist must function as an observing ego. In practical terms this means that with such a patient the therapist will be making many explicit references to the particular patient behaviors and thoughts that are mandating the contractual arrangement under discussion. Such interventions are along the lines of: "Since you have just told me X, I foresee the possibility of Y occurring in the treatment. What would you think therefore might be a reasonable way to deal with that eventuality?" Returning to our case example:

> THERAPIST: Well, whatever, but it needs to be updated.
>
> PATIENT: I'm on it. I'm making sure 'cause I have to get . . .
>
> THERAPIST: *(Interrupting)* Obviously we don't get paid if it's . . .
>
> PATIENT: *(Interrupting)* Yeah, and I'm also thinking about myself too, 'cause I'm supposed to get my glasses. I can't see. And I couldn't get them.
>
> THERAPIST: If you're not eligible for Medicaid, I don't know if it is or it isn't . . .
>
> PATIENT: *(Interrupting)* No, I'm eligible. It's just a mixup.
>
> THERAPIST: But if it turned out that for whatever reason you are not eligible for it, it would be your responsibility . . .
>
> PATIENT: *(Interrupting)* Right.
>
> THERAPIST: . . . to go to Ms. Smith and work out a payment . . .
>
> PATIENT: *(Interrupting)* Right.
>
> THERAPIST: . . . schedule. And at that time we would expect you to pay for all sessions.
>
> PATIENT: Right.
>
> THERAPIST: We would expect payment by the end of each month for the previous month. We would expect payment by the middle . . .
>
> PATIENT: *(Interrupting)* Right.
>
> THERAPIST: . . . of the next month. If that didn't happen we certainly would need to talk about that.
>
> PATIENT: Uh hm.
>
> THERAPIST: And if there would be a prolonged period of time when you didn't pay your bills, we would need to terminate the treatment.

Comment

The therapist has made a series of legislative statements, each of which the patient has responded to by interrupting and saying, "Right." The patient's response to the therapist's pontifications is to make clear both that she is only half listening to her and that she is caricaturing the agreement. When the therapist announces that, "If there would be a prolonged period of time when you didn't pay your bills, we would need to terminate the treatment," the tone of the remark as well as its context make it a threat rather than the inevitable outcome of the patient's actions. Alternatively, the therapist might have first responded to the patient's repeatedly saying "Right" with:

> I've noticed that as I've discussed the fee with you, you've responded as if you were impatient to get on with it, while, at the same time, appeared not to take the issue seriously. I don't know whether I'm correct about that or not, but assuming that there is some validity to my notion, it is conceivable that over time your failure to attend to the bill might well be your way of ending the treatment. In fact, doing self-destructive things that initially appear to you as ways of getting away with something is a pattern in your life that you told me is habitual for you.

By presenting the comment in this way, the therapist would accomplish several things: she would make the termination of the treatment the patient's responsibility by pointing out not that *"we* would need to terminate the treatment," but rather that the patient would be ending the therapy. Also, the therapist would empathically identify what it is about the patient's history that could lead one reasonably to assume that such behavior might reoccur. Finally, by underscoring how such behavior would be ultimately self-destructive, the therapist would appeal to that part of the patient that actively seeks collaboration.

PATIENT: There's no problem with that. I'm paying bills *(chuckling).*
THERAPIST: So again to make sure your Medicaid is up-to-date . . .
PATIENT: Uh hm.
THERAPIST: If that's not the case for a prolonged period of time, you would certainly need to bring that up because that would be clearly a problem . . .
PATIENT: *(Interrupting)* Uh hm.
THERAPIST: . . . in your treatment. If you're not up-to-date, you

need to work out a payment schedule. The other thing is that
even if you miss sessions, we still expect . . .

PATIENT: *(Interrupting)* Right.

THERAPIST: . . . payment. This is your time and we would expect
payment for this time.*

PATIENT: Right.

THERAPIST: The other thing is basically that we expect you to talk
freely and openly and honestly about your problems and difficulties that you're currently having. If there aren't any pressing
problems or difficulties, you are to talk freely and openly about
anything that comes to mind.

PATIENT: Uh hm.

THERAPIST: And that should include any memories, perceptions,
questions, or just anything that comes to your mind. If you're
able to do this, what's important will emerge very naturally.

PATIENT: Yeah.

THERAPIST: The important things that are going on inside of you
will surface. Regardless of how trivial you think the matter is, it's
still important to bring those things up in as open and honest
and free a way as possible. So, those are basically your responsibilities *(pause).* I'd like you to tell me what your understanding
of those things is, to repeat them back to me. I want to make
sure that you really heard what I had to say about what your
responsibilities are.

Comment

The therapist has detailed the ideal patient attitude and behavior regarding free and uncensored communications in the therapy. Her presentation ("what's important will emerge very naturally") failed to recognize
that this difficult type of communication is a goal that a patient usually
must work toward. To present this expectation as an actual state that
must be perfectly adhered to from the inception may project a sense of
rigidity in the therapy, which goes against the expectation of open
communication. What is required for the therapy to proceed at this point
is the patient's commitment to make every effort to communicate in this

*It is not clear whether the therapist does not know that Medicaid does not pay for
missed sessions or whether, in the context of this session, she has forgotten that fact.

way and to discuss her reluctance when she is encountering difficulties reporting her thoughts and feelings freely. A more complete statement would also include something like:

> Of course, speaking this freely is something that will not totally be within your grasp overnight, but it's something that together we can work toward. In the interim, it would be important for us to try to understand those instances in which you feel you cannot comply. Can you imagine any such instance at this point?

A more central deficiency in the earlier segment was the therapist's instructing the patient to repeat things back to her ("I want to make sure that you really heard what I had to say about what your responsibilities are"). It sounds like a test in which the professor-therapist quizzes the student-patient as to how effectively she has paid attention. This is not to say that the issue of whether the patient has attended to the therapist's statements is unimportant. On the contrary, it is crucial. The point is, as has been already mentioned several times, that the spirit of the inquiry needs to be dynamic rather than didactic or pedagogic. For example, after the patient has interrupted the therapist several times and announced "Right," the therapist might then raise the question, "Since you keep interrupting while seeming to agree, I wonder what reactions you are having to my articulating your responsibilities?" By evaluating the patient's investment in the task dynamically, the therapist facilitates the continuity between the contract phase and the treatment that may follow.

Conversely, a treatment that begins in the pedagogic fashion of this example would lend itself to struggles over authority and dependency. Note in the ensuing comments how the patient responds with an attitude of derision to increasing pressure from the therapist for a repetition of details. This attitude may be her way of protesting the therapist's didactic orientation.

PATIENT: Well, I'm supposed to be on time and make it to all the sessions, to pay, and to be honest.
THERAPIST: Can you give a little bit more detail? Remember what the first area of responsibility was?
PATIENT: It would start at 9:30 . . .

THERAPIST: Right.

PATIENT: . . . and end at 10:15. I have to be on time. Which is all good because I used to have a problem about being on time *(chuckling)* and paying my bills *(chuckling . . . speaking with mock solemnity)*. I've got to pay my bills and be honest and not be manipulative and lie and stuff like that *(pause)*. I understood what you said.

THERAPIST: What was your understanding about how many days a week?

PATIENT: Twice a week.

THERAPIST: Twice a week. You know which days?

PATIENT: Mondays and Thursdays, 9:30 to a quarter after ten.

THERAPIST: I just wanted to make sure . . .

PATIENT: Yeah *(laughing)*.

THERAPIST: . . . that we're on the same wave length.

PATIENT: *(Laughing)* We are.

THERAPIST: I want to be really sure that you understand that. There was one other thing which we'll talk about and then let's go over it again because I want you to really understand what the contract is. The session will start and end on time and also you need to make sure that you stay.

PATIENT: I wouldn't walk out anyway unless you really pissed me off. *(Laughing)* And I doubt it would happen, so I wouldn't.

THERAPIST: Even in that case I would expect you to stay so we can talk about it.

PATIENT: Yeah.

THERAPIST: See what I'm saying? Regardless of what happens you would stay till the end so that we can talk about it. Is that clear?

PATIENT: *(Agreeing)*

THERAPIST: So again the sessions will go from 9:30 to 10:15 on Mondays and Thursdays. I expect you to be there on time, to not leave, to leave on time.

PATIENT: Right.

THERAPIST: What was your understanding?

PATIENT: What do you mean by understanding? I mean I understood exactly what you're saying.

THERAPIST: I'd like to hear it from you to make sure that we're understanding the same thing.

Comment

By now it is clear that the patient is ridiculing the therapist's obsessive preoccupation with details. What might such a focus suggest about the therapist's position? On the manifest level, the therapist wants to be reassured that the patient will do the "right thing," but paradoxically, by avoiding confronting the process taking place between them, she is creating the opposite effect. That is, by caricaturing the contractual process herself, she promotes negative participation from the patient.

True exploration of whether collaborative understanding is being achieved requires that the "music" of the session be taken into account as well as the words: "Though your words seem to be, 'yes, yes, anything you say doctor,' your laughter and interruptions make me wonder about how seriously you are taking what I am saying. Perhaps you are protesting the responsibilities I am describing or the way in which I am putting things?"

What might compel a therapist to respond in such a seemingly persecutory fashion, grilling the patient as to whether or not she's gotten it "right"? Obviously, she may be angry with the patient. However, in our experience with fledgling therapists, what frequently emerges in supervision is that they fail to recognize when the patient has, in fact, reached the point of agreement. The therapist's endless interrogations are to reassure herself that the patient is agreeing and they can move on.

This question of what is enough raises the more complicated issue of the ultimate purpose of the treatment contract phase. It would be naive to assume that the successful completion of a treatment contract requires a guarantee that perfect execution of the therapy will then follow. Rather, the treatment contract must point out those absolute conditions that, if transgressed, would render the treatment impossible (for example, attendance, payment), those conditions, based on the patient's history, that require specific contingencies and may threaten the viability of the treatment (such as frequent calls to the therapist between sessions, involving the therapist in suicide attempts), and those conditions that patient and therapist must be aware of and accept as essential goals within the treatment (for example, speaking freely without censoring). Enunciating these responsibilities at the outset provides a frame of reference to which the therapist can return should problems arise during the course of the treatment.

In this particular session, there is a schoolmarmish quality to the therapist's exhortations of the patient, and a demand on her for a degree of reassurance that is impossible to attain. The nature of the psychodynamic process relies heavily on the elaboration of ambiguity and its subsequent analysis. There is a danger here that, by demanding such instant precision, the therapist will discourage the patient from exposing her uncertainty later on.

> PATIENT: Yeah, I have to pay the bills even if I don't make it to a session. I've got to make sure my Medicaid card's valid, and if not, then I have to make up a payment plan. It all makes sense 'cause this is like life. I've got to do these things anyway, so I have to be open and honest in sessions too. If I act that way here then it'll probably be a good foundation to act that way on the outside also.
>
> THERAPIST: That's the idea, yes.
>
> PATIENT: Yeah, so I understand it.
>
> THERAPIST: Also, that you're to talk openly and honestly about your difficulties and problems and, if you have nothing to say, then you talk about whatever comes to your mind.
>
> PATIENT: Yeah. Don't worry. You can't shut me up, so (laughing) no problem. I just have one question. What if I ever feel like I really don't need therapy anymore? I'm just saying, in the future. How about that?
>
> THERAPIST: That's something we need to discuss.
>
> PATIENT: All right.
>
> THERAPIST: That's something that I'd want you to bring into the session and then we could talk about it.
>
> PATIENT: OK. 'Cause I don't want to have it for the rest of my life. I know a lot of people do. But I don't want it for the rest of my life.

Comment

One wonders whether part of the patient's mockery might be related to her fear of being committed "for the rest of my life." Since one of the goals of the contract-setting phase is to underscore that the therapist's interventions are guided and informed by the patient's contribution, the therapist might have said, "Though this is an issue to be discussed in treatment, it may be that your concerns about being in treatment for the rest of your life are getting played out right now by your acting as if it's hard for you to take some of what we're talking about seriously."

> THERAPIST: It's not the intention of this work to have you here the rest of your life. It is a place for you to talk about your problems and difficulties and hopefully to gain a better understanding of yourself. That's the point of the treatment. Is that your understanding of what you wanted?

Comment

As has been said already, it is preferable for the therapist to elicit first what the patient wants. Here the therapist reverses the preferred order by first informing the patient of what the intention of the therapy is and *then* inquiring, "Is that your understanding of what you wanted?"

> PATIENT: Yeah. I don't mind that. My views are a little bit different than straight psychology. I don't want just to know about myself, I want to know about myself in relationship to how I relate to God and what He wants to do, and the work I want to do for Him, and stuff like that. My big thing is that I'm not sure you can understand me all the time. I've been thinking about that lately, I have a feeling you're not *(laughs)* . . . I don't want you to think I'm nuts or a fanatic, but I just don't think I'm going to really be understood by you all the time.
>
> THERAPIST: If I don't understand you, I'm going to ask you.
>
> PATIENT: Right. Just don't get me mad when you ask me *(laughing)*. I'm still very defensive *(laughing)*.
>
> THERAPIST: If I don't understand something, I'll simply ask. Hopefully you'll clarify things.
>
> PATIENT: OK.
>
> THERAPIST: So in terms of those first three things, why don't you just go through them once more?

Comment

The therapist again asks the patient to perform a sterile ritual immediately following the patient's having expressed fear that the therapist might think that she was "nuts or a fanatic," and that the therapist might not understand her and/or might get mad at her. The therapist's pedantic request for yet another review underscores the dissonance of the interaction. The patient speaks about fear while the therapist demands a more perfect performance.

PATIENT: OK. Be here at 9:30. We're going to end at 10:15. If I ever get upset in the middle of a session, not to walk out. I have to stay to the end. Start on time, end on time. Got to pay my bills. If I can't pay my bills, then I've got to make up a payment plan with Ms. Smith. I have to make sure my Medicaid card's valid.

THERAPIST: What does a payment plan mean?

PATIENT: Wouldn't it work that way if I don't have money to pay you?

THERAPIST: In the clinic you would work out what you could afford to pay.

PATIENT: Oh, all right.

THERAPIST: Whatever that is.

PATIENT: Then I pay that every week.

THERAPIST: You'd have to pay not every week, once a month.

PATIENT: Once a month. Oh, good; alright.

THERAPIST: It would be once a month. You'd get a bill for the previous month. For example, we meet twice a week so it would be eight sessions. You'd get a bill for eight sessions, eight times whatever that is and say this is January we're talking about, OK? So on February 1st you'd get a bill for eight sessions.

PATIENT: Right.

THERAPIST: And you would have until the fifteenth of February to pay that bill.

PATIENT: OK.

THERAPIST: That's to be paid to the clinic. If you would go beyond that then, that's something that clearly would be a problem in terms of the treatment. Hopefully you would even bring that up,

134

but I clearly would. That's something we would clearly need to talk about.

Comment

The therapist once again makes reference to "something we would clearly need to talk about." If there is such clarity about what needs to be talked about, why bring it up? If indeed the behavior that is being commented on is obvious, then reiterating it becomes an exercise in pedantry and, as such, devitalizes the work. More likely, the therapist is hoping that saying what the ideal scenario would be will magically make it happen. In fact, it is not clear to the therapist that the patient either would know this or, even if she did, would take the responsibility for raising it as an issue. In that case the therapist might say, "It's conceivable that the same reasons that would result in your not paying the bill would also cause you to overlook wanting to discuss this as an issue."

PATIENT: Yeah, I'm going to pay, don't worry *(laughing)*. You want to hear something good? Remember I told you about my one, big, gigantic outstanding bill with Altman's. Did I ever tell you that? I owe them $725.

THERAPIST: Hmm.

PATIENT: I wrote them a letter Friday. I told them I didn't realize it was two years, but it's been two years and I want to start paying it back. How about $10 a month or whatever they deem reasonable? I'll pay it once a month. I asked them to write back to tell me how they want to do it. I want to pay them.

THERAPIST: Good. Same principle applies here. You know you're here for a service you need to . . .

PATIENT: *(Interrupting)* Pay.

Comment

The therapist again demonstrates her need to be in control. She makes the link between Altman's and the therapy, rather than asking the patient if she can see a connection. The most important information is not that the two are linked, but rather how they are linked in the patient's mind. The therapist precludes any such exploration when she instructs the patient as to their similarity ("The same principle applies here. You know you are here for a service"). We don't know that the patient knows she's here for a service. The patient had introduced the Altman's story by first reassuring the therapist, "Don't worry," then laughing and asking her if she wanted to "hear something good." The patient seemed to be mocking Altman's and perhaps putting the therapist on notice as to her intentions vis-à-vis her services as well. The therapist intuitively notes the patient's aggression and attempts to override it via a superego appeal ("same principle applies here"), rather than encouraging the patient to elaborate her objections.

> THERAPIST: . . . pay your bills in a timely fashion. Why don't you say what the third thing is and then we'll go over it again.
> PATIENT: I have to go over it again? *(Chuckling, in a droning voice)* Be open and talk in therapy even if I don't have anything to talk about, talk as freely as I can, and just let things come out naturally in therapy.
> THERAPIST: The only other thing you would add is that we'll meet on Mondays and Thursdays.
> PATIENT: Yeah.
> THERAPIST: Why don't we go through it again and then this time I'm going to ask you if you actually agree with those things.
> PATIENT: OK, I just feel like I'm being treated retarded, but OK *(laughs)*. Um.

Comment

The therapist now reveals that having the patient repeat what she has said has served some function other than to establish whether the patient "actually agrees with those things." The patient appropriately responds that she feels as if she is being treated like a "retarded" person. The therapist's efforts up to this point have focused solely on whether she has been heard.

Though it is important to establish that the patient has listened and takes the task seriously, being able to echo back what the therapist says is a superficial and ineffective way to evaluate that. The therapist's own uncertainty about whether what she is saying is worth hearing might be the motivation for such an inquiry. It is also possible that her repeated inquiry may represent an attack on the patient and/or on the research project that teaches this model of therapy. Indeed, in a concordant identification with the patient (Racker, 1957), the therapist's caricaturing of the contract-setting phase may reflect her feeling that her participation in this process is at the expense of her own vitality.

> THERAPIST: Well, I'm not trying to make you feel retarded, I just want to make sure that we are totally . . .
> PATIENT: *(Interrupting)* We are *(laughs)*.
> THERAPIST: . . . crystal clear about . . .
> PATIENT: *(Interrupting)* I am *(laughing)*.
> THERAPIST: . . . what is expected . . .
> PATIENT: OK.
> THERAPIST: . . . of you and I want to make sure that you totally understand what's expected of me, so we'll go through this again. I think that it's important for the rest of the treatment that we totally understand each other in this regard.

Comment

There is an irony in the therapist's insisting that she wants to "make sure that you totally understand what's expected of me." Given that the therapist has failed to respond to the patient's repeated interruptions, caustic comments, and derisive laughter, the patient's understanding of what the therapist expects of herself may well be that she will carry out her task independent of the patient's input.

The therapist twice speaks of the need to "totally understand each other." No therapist-patient interaction is characterized by total understanding. In fact, it is precisely in examining those areas in which misunderstanding is felt to occur that the greatest therapeutic work is often done. Why is the therapist so burdened, and therefore burdening her patient, with a demand for total understanding? The therapist appears encumbered by a notion that all loose ends must be wrapped up in the contract-setting stage. Part of her must recognize that what she is insisting on is impossible. On a conscious level she continues to adhere to her absolute goal, admonishing the patient (by insisting on the repetition) for not reaching that goal, while unconsciously feeling frustrated by the impossible demand she is placing on herself and on the patient.

What this young therapist could most profit from would be a supervisor familiar with the principles of treatment contracting who would help her appreciate that the contract-setting phase is for establishing a frame within which to strive toward a goal rather than for achieving the goal in advance. The supervisor's task would also include helping the therapist appreciate how she might act out her failure to accept the limitations inherent in the treatment process by becoming increasingly demanding of the patient.

PATIENT: OK *(laughing).*
THERAPIST: All right? So?
PATIENT: You're not going to take my word for it huh? *(Laughing)*
THERAPIST: What do you mean?
PATIENT: I understand you *(laughing)* and I agree with everything.

Comment

The process has reached the point where patient and therapist are locked in a struggle about credibility. Note how far the patient's statement, "You're not going to take my word for it?" is from an emphasis on understanding and collaboration. The interview has taken on the atmosphere of a courtroom in which questions about rules of evidence and credibility dominate. This atmosphere provides data about issues within the field of the transference and countertransference; however, because the therapy has not yet begun and the therapist is not maintaining a position of neutrality, it is difficult to determine how to understand the data.

The therapist's repeated emphasis on pinning down an absolute commitment conveys the expectation that complex issues and feelings can be reduced to black-and-white terms and that there should be neither behavioral *nor* attitudinal differences between patient and therapist. In this context the patient says with exasperation, "I understand you and I agree with everything." When the contract is most successfully negotiated, the agreement as to behaviors within the context of treatment makes it possible to investigate the patient's underlying attitudes and assumptions that are in conflict with these behaviors.

THERAPIST: I understand you. You say you understand. I want to make sure we understand the same thing. That's what I want to be clear about.

PATIENT: OK.

THERAPIST: Let me go for one more time.

PATIENT: OK *(speaking mechanically)*. Got to meet here at 9:30 on Mondays and Thursdays.

THERAPIST: In my office, by the way.

Comment

The therapist's emphasis on absolutes has its analogue in her obsessive preoccupation with every last detail as, for example, when she finishes the patient's recitation of the meeting times by adding, "in my office, by the way." We do not know if "by the way" is the therapist's recognition, however unconscious, that this is indeed an incidental point and that she is caught up in a process beyond her conscious control, or whether the "by the way" is further expression of her anger at either the patient or the process. There is some suggestion that the therapist is, on some level, aware of her aggression and attempting to include the patient in the process when she petitions the patient to allow her to continue the interrogation: "Let me go for one more time."

PATIENT: Yeah.

THERAPIST: Yeah, OK.

PATIENT: And I've got to be on time and we're going to end on time at a quarter after ten and if I get upset I'm not to leave. I'm to wait it out and talk it through. I'm not to stay beyond the time of the session either.

THERAPIST: All right. Do you agree to that?

PATIENT: Yeah.

THERAPIST: That's OK with you?

PATIENT: Yeah.

THERAPIST: OK. You have no problem with that? OK. Go ahead.

PATIENT: I have to pay my bills and I have to make sure my Medicaid card is valid, and if it's not valid I have to get right on it and go down to talk to Ms. Smith. If I have to pay cash, I have to work out a payment plan and pay once a month and just make sure that I keep up on my bills. I didn't know about checking in with my Medicaid card, so I'll do that every week now also.

THERAPIST: And the payment is to be in by the middle of the next . . .

PATIENT: Right. By the 15th.

THERAPIST: Are you in agreement with that? Do you have a problem with any of that?

PATIENT: Nope.

THERAPIST: You don't have a problem. OK, and . . .

PATIENT: *(Interrupting)* I have to be honest in therapy, be open, and if I have nothing to talk about, talk as freely as I can about anything and things will naturally progress from there. And just utilize my therapy time 'cause I got to pay for it anyway.

THERAPIST: To talk is to talk about your difficulties and problems that you're having, and if you're not having any at the moment, to talk as freely and openly as you can.

PATIENT: I agree.

THERAPIST: Do you have a problem with any of that?

PATIENT: No.

Comment

By this point the patient's responses appear as mechanical as the interviewer's questions. Each participant manifests her aggression through the use of words as ritual, destroying the communication of meaning and replacing it with noise. Given the problems borderline patients have managing their aggression, the patient is "learning" a style of dealing with aggression through a mocking identification with the therapist.

THERAPIST: OK, fine. OK. Let's go to my responsibilities. My responsibilities are to be there for these two sessions a week, to be there on time, which again is Mondays and Thursdays at 9:30, to be there at 9:30 till 10:15. That's one important part of my job. The other is that if I'm going to be away, I give you plenty of notice, several weeks notice about that.

PATIENT: When you go away, you're not going to act as though that's the be-all and end-all of my life? I had this therapist once—this gets me really mad—she acted as though because she went away on vacation that I was supposed to crumple and die. Don't act like that with me because that will get me very mad *(laughs)*. OK?

THERAPIST: Your therapist acted as if . . .

PATIENT: *(Interrupting)* Everything, every problem that I had or anything I talked about, she believed stemmed from the fact that she went away on vacation for a week! She believed I wasn't expressing my pent up, um, frustrations about her going away and feeling abandoned by her. That's my big beef against psychiatrists.

THERAPIST: I can't make any predetermined notions about what I may or may not say.

PATIENT: Just keep it in the back of your mind *(laughing)*.

Comment

The patient is warning her therapist not to consider herself the center of the patient's universe. The contract-setting phase has taken on an oppositional pattern in which each participant warns the other about the dangers that may follow, should they work together. The patient, in predicting that all her feelings about the therapist arise as a reaction to the therapist's actual behavior, leaves no room for her to consider the impact of transference, of what she "reads into" the situation between her and the therapist.

This prediction may be a reflection of the immediate situation. As the therapist bears down on the patient about her understanding of the conditions of treatment, the patient becomes more likely to be convinced that her own feelings are an objective response to the therapist's behavior and less likely to be open to the possibility these feelings may include an element of transference. Since borderline patients often have trouble with self-object differentiation and, therefore, with appreciating transference, it is especially unfortunate that this therapist's own actions have made the idea of any transferential aspect even more difficult for the patient to consider.

THERAPIST: If I felt that was going on, I would need to tell you. It would be honest on my part to do so.

141

Comment

The therapist's statement that honesty would compel her to inform the patient of any attitude she might hold toward her reflects the therapist's lack of appreciation of what it means to be "in role." Therapists must utilize their reactions as a crucial source of data about the patient. Part of that process includes deciding which information to communicate and when to do it. The idea that "the principle of honesty compels me to . . ." deprives therapists of their right and responsibility to make that choice. Further, therapists who are struggling with countertransference issues of guilt can, under the banner of total disclosure, exploit their patient by making confessions so as to compel the patient to absolve them—or, alternatively, therapists experiencing anger in the countertransference can, under the same banner, act out the anger through excessively blunt "honest" reactions.

PATIENT: But if I felt that, I would tell you too.

THERAPIST: I would hope you would.

PATIENT: It bothers me when the psychiatrists think they're your lifeline. I feel it's demeaning.

THERAPIST: Well, it sounds like that's an issue to talk about in treatment. That leads me to the third part of my responsibility, which is to listen to you as you talk about your problems and whatever else comes to your mind. It's going to be my job to listen very attentively to you and to try to help you understand what's going on inside of you. In general I'm going to be quieter than I have been during the history taking. If I feel I have something to contribute, I'll make a comment. If not, I won't say anything. The material from which I work is based on what you have to say.

PATIENT: I guess what I mean is just don't make stupid assumptions *(laughing)*. I think that's more or less what it was; it was just a stupid assumption.

THERAPIST: Do you feel that I'm making a stupid assumption if I help you bring that issue up?

PATIENT: I probably will *(laughing)*.

THERAPIST: OK. Let's go through my responsibilities.

PATIENT: OK. You have to be on time, just as I have to be on time.

That's twice a week at 9:30 to a quarter after ten. You can't leave if I piss you off *(laughing)*. I'm only kidding.

THERAPIST: Well that's part of it. I can't, I won't leave. I will be there.

PATIENT: You have to tell me well in advance when you're going on vacation. You're not going to make any stupid assumptions, and if you do, I get to call you on it. And you're going to listen to what I have to say.

Comment

The patient has announced that the therapist "can't leave" if the patient makes her angry, and the therapist initially concurs with "I can't," which she then changes to "won't." However, her initial statement of agreement seems more accurate since the entire tone of the session has been to compel the two participants to bear some awful burden, as if they are to be chained together rather than freely joining one another. The tenor of the interview has facilitated an attitude of dutiful obedience, right and wrong, and reward and punishment. By contrast, a contract ought to ensure a background of mutual safety and predictability where retaliation is a fantasy to be analyzed rather than a fact to be endured.

The caricature of the treatment as a rigid absolute phenomenon is well captured by the patient's prescription, "You're not going to make any stupid assumptions," reflecting her implicit demand for a perfect therapist. The comment, "If you do [make stupid assumptions], I get to call you on it," indicates that the patient feels it is by a particular contractual arrangement that she is being allowed to react to the therapist's imperfections, rather than that the purpose of the contract is to guarantee that open and honest communication will take place at all times, irrespective of the particular issue at hand.

Case Study #2

In the session we will now turn to, as in the one just examined, the therapist fails to engage the patient actively in the process of contract setting; however, the two therapists are very different in their approach.

In the first interview the therapist's excessive repetition robbed the encounter of any life, and the therapist avoided confronting crucial objections raised by the patient. In the contract-setting interview that follows, the therapist has difficulty maintaining the process of contract setting with a patient who attempts to introduce treatment issues too rapidly—before there is an understanding about how the work will take place.

Borderline patients frequently express narcissistic entitlement and a wish for omnipotent control, making excessive demands on others, including their therapists, while acting as if ordinary social conventions do not apply to them. Therapists frequently get caught up in the dizzying challenges and invitations that these primitive patients offer and, in the process, forget their own limitations and requirements. Thus, it is not surprising that a therapist may rush in to rescue a patient before establishing that there is any basis for their working together. If the goal is to set up a long-term working relationship in which situations that currently manifest themselves as emergencies can eventually be identified and worked through, it is essential that there first be a mutually agreed upon set of ground rules. When therapists suspend the recognition that such a need exists, they join the patient in omnipotent fantasies, which will eventually doom the treatment. Attempting the impossible can only result in the treatment failing, the patient finding justification for her devaluing defenses, and her sense of isolation, burdensomeness, and destructive power being reinforced.

The interview begins with the therapist clarifying that the history-taking phase is over and that now is the time to discuss the contract.

PATIENT: Are we still working on history?

THERAPIST: No. Before we start the treatment, I think we need to work on how we are going to conduct it.

PATIENT: How we're going to conduct the treatment?

THERAPIST: We should have guidelines about how the treatment should be conducted. I'll have certain expectations about how the treatment can continue. I have certain responsibilities, as do you. We should discuss them thoroughly and see if those responsibilities can be met, and if so, then we could proceed with the treatment. We first have to clarify how we shall be conducting the treatment.

Comment

The therapist's initial statement about the contract setting is confusing. He says, "We should have guidelines about how the treatment should be conducted," rather than "The treatment has certain guidelines." Since he has not first discussed the nature of the treatment, his statement suggests either that the guidelines are independent of the treatment or that they arise out of the therapist's idiosyncratic perspective. The latter idea is reinforced by the therapist's saying, "*I'll* have certain expectations about how the treatment can continue."

Rather than the therapist deciding "how the treatment should be conducted," each particular treatment has certain basic properties that define its character. For example, in psychodynamic psychotherapy both parties must be present if the treatment is to take place.* While this may sound obvious, it often becomes an issue, given both the various obstacles that can arise in relation to the parties' ability to be present and the many forms that resistance can take. Nonetheless, both participants must be there, not because of a whim of the therapist, but because of the nature of the psychodynamic treatment process. It is especially important for therapists working with borderline patients to appreciate this distinction since frequently the patient will attack her therapist for employing rules "for your own good." By understanding that these principles exist to safeguard the work of the therapy, the therapist can maintain sufficient distance to examine the patient's charge of selfish motivation.

This therapist's statement suggests confusion about whether he is doing an evaluation or has already obligated himself to the treatment, particularly when he speaks of having expectations "about how the treatment can continue" and when he says, "Then we could proceed with the treatment."

PATIENT: I don't really know, to tell you the truth. We're going to meet a couple of times a week but other than that I'm not sure. I was going to ask you again last night and again today about

---

*In other therapies where there is not a high priority on using words instead of action, and where analysis of resistance is not part of the treatment process, it may be quite appropriate for the patient to decide not to come or for the therapist to call the patient to discuss medication management, and so forth.

maybe starting on an antidepressant because I still felt kind of in the doldrums. I know drinking hasn't helped that, and I have found it difficult to stop drinking.

Comment

The patient merely pays lip service to considering the therapist's request to discuss the conditions of treatment as she immediately attempts to involve him in a treatment issue. She even suggests a subtle form of bribery, intimating that if the therapist gives her an antidepressant, she will discontinue self-medication with alcohol.

> THERAPIST: There are two things here. We can assess whether we should consider an antidepressant, but I also think your drinking is an important issue as well. You have a history of drinking and continue to drink, and that can impact here on the treatment. Let me go over some basic guidelines for the treatment. It's expected that you will come in twice a week and that we'll need to work out regular times for those sessions. It's important that we have our full amount of time so we can work on the difficulties you have. You mentioned drinking and how you continue to drink. It's quite important that you come here as alert as possible because the work is difficult, and anything that can interfere with your alertness is going to greatly interfere with what we do here. Drinking is one of many things that would interfere with that. It's not possible to work this way if you are at all intoxicated by alcohol or anything else. What we will have to do if you do come here intoxicated is to terminate the session and meet for a regular session the next time. Should you no longer be intoxicated, we can then continue our work. We would want to look at why you came to the session intoxicated, but in fact, we would not be able to accomplish anything while you are intoxicated.

Comment

The therapist is not opposed to drinking on either moral or medical grounds. The problem is that since this therapy places a premium on reflection, anything that reduces the capacity to do so diminishes its effectiveness.

The therapist could make it even more explicit that it is the patient who poses a threat to the treatment rather than that the therapist is making a demand. He might say, "If you come drunk to a session, you will be making your participation impossible, and therefore it is you who will be ending the session. Should you make this a chronic pattern, then you will be destroying your treatment."

The therapist's comments identify the patient's behavior as destructive and, importantly, imply that change, through understanding, is possible ("We would want to look at why it is you came to the session intoxicated").

PATIENT: I've never had anything like that.

THERAPIST: The alcohol problem still seems quite active. You say so yourself.

PATIENT: I don't really know why, but it's harder to go out and not drink. Actually, I haven't really tried to stop. I'm sure one or two drinks aren't going to matter that much, and I'm sure it's just an excuse of sorts not to try and stop.

Comment

The patient focuses on the difficulty she has stopping drinking but not on how continuing to drink would affect her participation in treatment. While it may be difficult for her to withdraw from alcohol, that has nothing to do with whether an expressive psychotherapy can be conducted with an inebriated patient—it cannot. Understanding why a patient says she "cannot" do something, cannot stop drinking in this case, does not provide the therapist with a way to avoid a condition of treatment, sobriety, that is essential. Rescue fantasies, which borderline patients are especially adept at inducing, often distort good clinical judgment. Therapists may come to feel that they must find a way to overcome this or that requirement of the treatment, especially if their patient successfully appeals to their narcissism.

THERAPIST: Well?

PATIENT: Go ahead.

THERAPIST: OK. In the future we can look at what your drinking is about, but right now we are setting guidelines about how we can conduct this treatment. Being in an intoxicated state will have to stop. *(Pause)* I mentioned twice a week.

Comment

The patient has made clear that she hasn't "really tried to stop" and indicates she doesn't agree that there is necessarily any incompatibility between her having "one or two drinks" and treatment. The therapist speaks, however, as if the issue is settled when he says, "We are just setting guidelines about how we can conduct this treatment, so being in an intoxicated state will have to stop."

By failing to confront the patient with her clear-cut resistance, the therapist lends credibility to the patient's cavalier attitude. Essentially, the therapist is saying, "I'm going to pretend that I didn't hear you say you don't see the need for not drinking. Instead, I'll act as if my saying it will have to stop will make it happen." Paradoxically, by not taking the patient's words seriously, the therapist encourages the patient to take the same attitude toward his own statements. Once either party can comfortably ignore what the other has said, the value of all verbalization is put into question.

By immediately following his statement that intoxication makes therapy impossible with a discussion of appointment times, the therapist further undermines his own position. Instead, the therapist needed to confront the patient with how she deflected the discussion away from what the treatment requires and to examine the patient's belief that the therapist will figure out a way to circumvent his own recommendation. For example, the therapist might suggest that if the patient feels unable to stop drinking, she might first go to A.A. rather than therapy and, should she attain sobriety, then return to the therapist for further discussion about the possibility of working together.

By moving rapidly away from the patient's statement, the therapist does not take the patient seriously. By the same token the patient's refusal to engage the therapist in a discussion about the conflict between her wish to drink and her wish to be in treatment is her way of not taking the therapist seriously.

PATIENT: Regular times?

THERAPIST: We have to have regular times. Maybe that is something we can accomplish right now. That's been difficult for you to do. You've already cancelled a number of times, and we'll have to discuss how that takes place.

PATIENT: I try to reschedule when I have to cancel, but I had to go out of town for work. Yesterday I had train trouble. Now I am moving to the city. I just got an apartment yesterday. We're going to have to think up an appointment for early mornings or later evenings.

Comment

As with the drinking, the issue that requires attention here is the patient's belief that therapy can go on despite her absence, not her reasons for not coming. It is one thing for the patient to wish for an omniscient therapist who can know the patient even when she is not there; it is another thing to convert that fantasy into a real demand of her therapist. When describing any condition necessary for treatment, it is important to acknowledge to the patient that she may find compliance difficult and to anticipate with her why the difficulties may occur. For example, "I understand that you have a variety of transportation problems that make it difficult for you to come to sessions; however, my understanding that does not make the problem of your needing to be here go away."

THERAPIST: I can offer you this time on a regular basis. Tuesdays at 4:30. We can have Tuesday and Friday as our regular times at 4:30 in the afternoon.

PATIENT: So that is it. Once we get in here, what does therapy consist of, just hashing it out *(laughing)*, talking about things? I don't know exactly what it's about—are there guidelines that need to be set?

THERAPIST: Yes. There are several more before we get into what we will be doing here. We need to set up some contracts around other behaviors as well. You very recently made a serious

suicide attempt. It was very near being lethal, in fact it's, it's
. . . you are quite lucky that you are still alive. What we need
to do is to work out how you are going to deal with your
impulsive behavior and how that is going to impact on the
treatment.

The patient makes a good point when she asks, "What does the
therapy consist of?" before inquiring about guidelines. As previously
discussed, only those guidelines that derive directly from the requirements of the particular therapy being considered are necessary. Guidelines that do not evolve directly out of the needs of the treatment
process are vulnerable to being influenced by countertransference. For
example, if, as this patient suggests, one were to engage in a "hashing
out" therapy, a process primarily utilizing catharsis and reality testing,
it would not be necessary for the therapist to set up guidelines to protect
his technical neutrality.

Unfortunately, the therapist's very next comment underscores his
lack of understanding that the guidelines should evolve from the treatment. He announces that "There are several more [contractual issues]
before we get into what we will be doing here." When the rules do not
derive from the treatment, they tend to take on a life of their own and
sound preachy. For example, the therapist's comment that the patient is,
in fact, "quite lucky" to still be alive is both a warning and a judgment.
His statement makes it more difficult for the patient to consider that the
therapist could be interested in understanding her feeling unlucky to be
alive or her positive fantasies regarding death. A more neutral statement
would be, "Killing yourself is the ultimate act of making the treatment
impossible." In this statement, the therapist is not favoring the expression of one aspect of the patient over another, but is indicating an
alliance with the treatment being offered to the health-seeking part of
the patient.

PATIENT: I think staying off the alcohol and keeping on a regular
schedule will help anything impulsive. And that is that.
THERAPIST: But at the same time it seems difficult for you to control
the alcohol.
PATIENT: I can only try another week of telling myself that I won't
do it and see how I do. We meet again Tuesday and I'll find out

how I've done over this weekend. I think it will be all right. It will be about five days that I've put effort into stopping.

THERAPIST: My thoughts were that if you are feeling impulsive and have used your normal routes of trying to get help, it's quite important for you to call me before you act on any impulse to kill yourself.

PATIENT: I haven't even thought about it in a long time even though things have been bad. I just think about what other alternative can I do to get out of this. I haven't really thought, "I wish I could kill myself," at all. That's how I had been thinking about up to three weeks ago. I haven't thought about it lately.

THERAPIST: Given that you've tried to kill yourself several times already, it would be surprising if you didn't have thoughts of doing it again.

PATIENT: No. It surprised me that I haven't even thought about it lately.

THERAPIST: All the more reason for us to work out a way of dealing with this now.

PATIENT: If I thought about it.

Comment

A number of things require comment here. First, the therapist's inviting the patient to call him undermines the principle that the patient take responsibility for herself and that the therapeutic interaction be limited to sessions times. Second, the patient's comment that she is "surprised" by her not having thought about suicide lately indicates she is, on some level, struggling with it. Third, when a patient readily acquiesces to a therapist's clarification about a contractual issue or fails to identify any conflict within herself, the therapist should probe further. He might say, "How can we understand that suddenly you find it so easy to abandon something that's been so central in your life?"

THERAPIST: Optimally you would be able to contain your impulse and wait for our session to discuss it. If that is not possible, it would be important for you to call someone to discuss it. That certainly can include me. If I feel that you are abusing the telephone, we can discuss that as well.

Comment

If the patient intrudes on the therapist's life outside the session, that might compromise his ability to be open to the patient's productions during sessions. Therefore, it would be preferable for the therapist to comment on how unwarranted phone calls might impede his ability to listen objectively rather than to refer to the vaguer and more moralistic notion of "abuse." By situating the need for the limit in the context of safeguarding the climate of the therapy, he would be addressing an outcome that, in theory at least, is desired by both of them.

> PATIENT: What do you mean by "abusing the telephone"? If there are too many calls?
>
> THERAPIST: Yes. Or if it doesn't feel like an emergency, we can discuss that as well. Should you find that you are unable to control your impulse to hurt yourself or if you have already done something, it is imperative that you go to a hospital, and then they can evaluate you and treat you if necessary. They'll make the decisions about the need for hospitalization, and once you are discharged, we can continue our treatment.
>
> PATIENT: I haven't felt impulsive. I haven't even thought about it. Just yesterday I was thinking that it was an improvement that I hadn't thought about suicide in a while. I don't know what made me think about not having thought about it. Maybe it was something on TV or a movie or just hearing the word some-where else.
>
> THERAPIST: Two things come to mind. First, you did start the session asking for antidepressants?
>
> PATIENT: Uh huh.
>
> THERAPIST: So, you must still be feeling badly if you are asking for them. It wouldn't be surprising given the number of times you have tried to commit suicide. I recall your overdosing as well as cutting yourself with razors. It's also going to be difficult for you to communicate this because the way you previously behaved was not to tell anyone.
>
> PATIENT: I felt like it's a really awful thing to think about, to bring out in the open. It's just not something worth discussing. *(Pause)* I was at a party and somebody asked me, "Did you try to burn

yourself?" I thought it was kind of funny that somebody was able to say something about it, able to admit it. Most of the other people just said they were glad I was back. Nobody really talked about it. Nobody would quite talk about feeling down and things like that, or that they thought about it before too. It doesn't seem like something to discuss.

THERAPIST: I would expect that we will be discussing this a fair amount. It is your responsibility to bring it up.

PATIENT: Uh huh.

THERAPIST: Uh, in addition, we haven't clarified the fee.

Comment

The patient comments that her self-destructiveness is not "worth discussing" and twice says that people have reacted negatively to her efforts to talk about suicide: "Nobody really talked about it." The patient's references to other people's avoidance could easily reflect her sense of the interviewer who avoids confronting the patient with her indecision about whether to continue to live and who moves rapidly from a discussion of suicide to a statement about his fee, as if they were equivalent issues.

PATIENT: Uh.

THERAPIST: From the last time we met, I understand that you were told that this would be free because it's a research project.

PATIENT: And Medicare or Medicaid would cover this.

THERAPIST: It's my feeling that we should work out a fee. We have the unusual ability to be able to work out a fee that you could afford, but I think it's quite important that you pay a fee, that you take responsibility for this treatment in a number of ways, including payment of a fee.

PATIENT: I really don't have an income. This weekend is the first time I worked for a while. Prior to that I only had an income of about $150 a week, so I don't really know how you're going to slide the scale unless it's $20 a session or something like that.

THERAPIST: How much will you be making?

PATIENT: I have no idea.

THERAPIST: You said you were just working?

PATIENT: I worked this weekend. I made about $3,000 but it doesn't mean that I know when I'm getting my next job or how much I will be getting over the year.

THERAPIST: In that case, knowing that your work is so intermittent, it will be important for you to put some money away so as to be able to pay on a regular basis.

PATIENT: Uh huh.

THERAPIST: Do you have any thoughts about what would be a realistic fee?

PATIENT: Based upon what I've done so far this year, I think that I don't know if I can afford more than $50 for the week. That would be $25 a session.

THERAPIST: What is your thought about that?

PATIENT: At this point it seems expensive. How much do you usually get? I don't know what's fair anyway. You think it's more motivating if I am paying for it?

THERAPIST: It's more than it's just motivating. There's research to show that people who do not pay for their treatment do not do as well as people who do pay. I don't think it is in your interest to have to start a treatment that is already flawed and that won't give you the benefit that another treatment will.

Comment

The therapist appeals to science to make his point, indicating that there is "research to show" the value of paying for treatment. This appeal to an external authority indicates his discomfort with letting the material speak for itself and/or having the patient challenge him. The therapist's resorting to external authority may also reflect his own lack of clarity about the merit of having the patient pay for her treatment. There is a minor irony here in that the therapist focuses on the fee as evidence of the patient's taking responsibility for her treatment and, by extension, her life, while failing to focus on the more direct issue of abdicating responsibility—whether she will commit suicide.

PATIENT: *(Pause)* All I know is that I can probably pay fifty bucks for the next month and then re-evaluate it after that.

THERAPIST: Let's go with that fee and we can re-evaluate it. Perhaps it should go even higher if your work is that consistent. You have the potential for a high income.

PATIENT: OK. Fine.

THERAPIST: Now, *(pause)* in addition, if for any reason you are unable to come to session, it's expected that you'll call to cancel the sessions.

PATIENT: I think I've been good about that so far, have I not? Except for last night.

THERAPIST: Uh huh.

PATIENT: The situation was such that I couldn't call right then. I did as soon as I could.

THERAPIST: Let me discuss your responsibility within the session to speak as freely as you can . . .

PATIENT: *(Interrupting)* It doesn't seem to be very free right now.

THERAPIST: . . . to speak as freely as you can, to say what is on your mind without screening or editing your thoughts. At times when you're not having a particular conflict, you may want to discuss some perceptions you have, something from a previous session, dream, or memory. It is imperative that you be as honest as you can be about what's on your mind and to speak about whatever you are experiencing here.

PATIENT: Right now I'm experiencing feeling uptight about not being able to do that. I don't know if and when I can break down the barrier and be able to do that. I don't know what it is, but something in me doesn't allow me to share my feelings or my thoughts.

Comment

In response to the therapist's statement that the patient will be expected to call to cancel, the patient responds as if her integrity is being questioned, "I think I've been good about that so far." A few moments later, the patient describes herself as not feeling "very free right now." While the sense of being persecuted may occur as a result of the patient's distortion, one must also consider that the therapist, by presenting the contract without acknowledging that there is room for ambiguity or differences of opinion and without having rooted the requirements of the therapy in the method of treatment, has facilitated the patient's feeling that she is on trial.

> THERAPIST: This is a difficulty that you have experienced for quite some time?
>
> PATIENT: I guess so. I felt that I went through *(sniffling)* through a period where I was very expressive, but I don't know what has happened that has made me completely closed off again. *(Sniffling)* I feel like I don't know. I just feel like I don't have anything to say. I just hate the situation I've been in lately. I've been feeling shitty about myself and I just drive myself down again and again instead of picking myself up. I'm drinking too much and not getting up and exercising.
>
> THERAPIST: These sound like things we ought to talk about, and they appear to be quite distressing to you.
>
> PATIENT: I guess so *(sniffling)*.
>
> THERAPIST: *(Pause)* We've discussed a number of things right now and I am wondering what your thoughts are about the guidelines that we are setting up for treatment.
>
> PATIENT: I just hope that I will be able to work enough to be able to pay. I think working enough will also lift my spirits a little bit. It will give me something to strive for instead of just sitting around all the time. As far as the times are concerned, I hope that the hours that I work are staggered enough, so I can be up at the job or wherever I have to be at the right time, since I will have to commute.

Comment

To a large extent, the patient's assessment that she can comply with the contract is based on faith. She "just hopes" that she will be able to pay for sessions and come to them on time. An element of doubt and ambivalence about any of the conditions of the contract is to be expected. Indeed, it is reassuring to hear a patient express some reservation. However, when the patient leaves everything to chance, it is as if the matter is outside her domain.

It would be important for the therapist to investigate actively with the patient what conditions she can identify within herself that might either facilitate or obstruct her participation. For example, the therapist might say, "Is there anything that you know about yourself that would indicate to you whether you will be able to and are interested in meeting these conditions? What can we learn about you that would suggest the likelihood of finding it difficult to follow the contract?"

Summary

Each of these sessions illustrates particular problems clinicians have in establishing a treatment contract. In the first session, the clinician, in collaboration with the patient, devitalizes the process to the point where it becomes a hollow ritual. The spirit of collaboration is sacrificed to the letter of forming an agreement; there is the sense of a technical, legalistic contract rather than a compact based on agreement in principle. In the second case, the clinician fails to make clear that the conditions for treatment emanate from the treatment process under consideration, reinforcing the patient's already existing sense that she is the recipient of unfair and arbitrary demands. In sum, as these two cases clearly demonstrate, establishing a treatment contract with a borderline patient is a complicated and subtle task. It requires constant sensitivity to the implications of the process unfolding between patient and therapist as well as to the content of the contract.

CHAPTER 7

The Contract as Reference Point in Later Phases of Treatment

IT WOULD BE NAÏVE to assume that once the treatment contract is set up, the therapy will unfold within the established frame without deviation. In this chapter we will review two cases. The first case will provide an overview of a patient's treatment history, following her course through three therapies with a focus on the degree of attention each therapist paid to carefully structuring the treatment and following the contract. Our review of the second case will focus on the development of the therapeutic dialogue and the role of repeated references to the contract in advancing the work of the treatment.

Case Study #1

The first case is that of a patient, N.S., later diagnosed as borderline, who initially sought therapy during her senior year of high school because of feelings of depression and anxiety. She began a twice-weekly supportive therapy with Mr. X. After six months of treatment focusing on understanding the relation of her mood to current stresses and past family situations, patient and therapist began to have sexual relations.

Soon thereafter, the patient began to live with Mr. X, who by then had left his wife and children. The two continued a stormy relationship for a number of years until Mr. X died in circumstances involving a degree of negligence of the part of N.S. Clearly the initial treatment in this case was lacking in structure to an extreme degree. From one point of view, the patient's chaotic inner dynamics were not contained by the therapy, but rather took over the situation and guided the events in the lives of the two parties involved.

After Mr. X's death, N.S. sought therapy a second time. She presented to Dr. Y, a psychiatrist, with complaints that now included alcohol abuse, anorexia nervosa, and such self-destructive behaviors as cutting herself with razor blades. She began therapy in conjunction with resuming her education at the college level. Her therapist framed a treatment with the goal of increasing the patient's level of functioning: a twice-weekly therapy based on discussion of the patient's difficulties and exploration of the role past events contributed to these difficulties. As the therapy progressed, the treatment goal became defined more specifically as helping the patient graduate from college in order to attend law school. Dr. Y agreed to let the patient call him in between sessions if she was having a difficult time and thought the phone contact would help her deal with the stress of her studies or preparing for an exam; he allowed her to page him at his hospital as a means of contacting him.

From a practical point of view, this therapy appeared to be succeeding. The patient passed her courses and was to graduate from college. She invited Dr. Y to her graduation. He agreed to attend. On graduation day, he went to the ceremony but, because of his busy schedule, left before its completion. N.S. reacted to Dr. Y's early departure from the ceremony by taking a large overdose of medication. She became comatose and remained in an intensive care unit for three days before regaining consciousness. This development suggests that the apparently successful therapy was seriously flawed. By addressing the patient's functioning at the expense of exploring the affects that emerged in the relationship with the therapist, both parties colluded in a pseudo-cure that sidestepped the patient's internal dynamics. Her functioning, bolstered by the support of the therapist, improved, but her character—her way of perceiving and responding to the world—did not.

After N.S.'s hospitalization, she began therapy with Dr. T, who prescribed a treatment with a carefully defined contract. During the first months, the treatment proceeded without drama but with concern on the part of Dr. T. N.S. had begun law school and devoted most of her time in session to discussing the stresses of that experience. Although Dr. T had defined the work of treatment as exploration of the patient's inner feelings and conflicts, the therapist sensed that N.S. was transforming their work into a repetition of the therapy with Dr. Y, with its focus on functioning at school. Yet Dr. T could not claim that the patient was abrogating their contractual agreement, since the discussion of problems at school involved looking at her feelings and inner conflicts.

The therapy continued for eight months, with Dr. T concerned that the central issues in the patient's pathology were not emerging in the treatment. Then, Dr. T noted a deviation in the contract and decided to explore it. N.S. mentioned in passing that she had received an unexpected inheritance from an aunt. Dr. T recalled to himself that the fee negotiated with the patient was set low because of her need to survive on student loans. It was understood that if her financial situation improved they would renegotiate the fee. He reminded her of this in session. N.S. reacted with rage. She accused him of avarice and selfishness. She attacked his professional values. She brought her criticisms of him beyond the boundaries of therapy by denouncing him at her A.A. meeting in a way that threatened to harm his reputation throughout the community.

Dr. T was aware that the storm of affect unleashed by directing the patient's attention to her deviation from the contract was the most important development in the therapy thus far. The treatment, which had seemed somewhat static until now, became intensely alive. N.S.'s affects and distortions were available to work with more directly than they had been heretofore. The transference was almost palpable. Dr. T repeatedly invited the patient to observe what she was experiencing within the therapy. N.S. initially rejected these invitations, claiming that there was nothing to learn. According to her, the situation was straightforward: Dr. T was interested only in exploiting her for financial gain, and his insistence that her reaction may have some meaning was a lie tailored to distract her from his true nature.

In spite of her insistence on the "straightforward" nature of the situation, N.S. continued to attend sessions. This suggested that she was willing gradually to consider alternate ways of understanding the situation. After almost two months of working on this deviation from the contract and all that it catalyzed, N.S. began to move beyond the position of projecting her own exploitativeness onto Dr. T and expressed some ability to consider alternate ways of understanding what had transpired. Ultimately she learned a great deal from this extended interaction and was able to express some gratitude to Dr. T for continuing to work on this issue as persistently as he had.

We have reviewed N.S.'s series of therapies to underline the importance of careful attention to the treatment contract in the treatment of borderline patients. This case illustrates the importance of the contract both in containing the patient's acting out and in maintaining the treatment focus on the transference so that the patient's dynamics will neither overwhelm the treatment situation nor be obscured by a more superficial focus.

Case Study #2

In this case the patient breached the contract in sessions from the start of therapy by remaining silent and not reporting her thoughts. While the goal of totally free expression of thoughts and feelings is acknowledged to be difficult and to require time to attain, the contract calls for consistent commitment and effort in working toward this goal. This patient's silence created a threat to the possibility of treatment. The therapist's early focus on these breaches provided an immediate opportunity to address the patient's chronic oppositionality and underlying paranoia and to begin to discern some of the projected part-object representations being activated in the sessions.

The case is that of a woman in her early thirties who meets all eight DSM-III-R criteria for Borderline Personality Disorder. Her history had been marked by multiple serious suicide attempts and many hospitalizations. She had had several prior psychotherapies, but no change in her suicidal behaviors. The therapy began with two history-taking sessions and a session that included the patient's parents. The therapist called for the latter because of his concern that the patient might indeed kill herself at some point and he wished to communicate to her parents, who were subsidizing the treatment, that although he was recommending this therapy he could not guarantee its success. He explained to them, as he had to her, that he did not feel hospitalization was indicated as a preferred form of treatment. Her suicidal impulses were chronic, a way of life for her, and only a long-term hospitalization, which was not a realistic option in this case, would have any chance of helping her achieve the necessary degree of character change in a safer setting.

Following these sessions, the therapist had planned to begin the contract-setting process. However, the patient missed the first planned contract-setting session because she had ingested poison and was hospitalized. She did not call the therapist to inform him of her actions or of the fact that she would not be attending the scheduled session. After she was cleared medically and discharged from the hospital, the patient attended the next session and resumed negotiation of the treatment with the therapist, who described and discussed the treatment contract with her during the next two sessions. In light of the patient's recent actions, the therapist emphasized that she would be responsible for informing him if she would not be attending a session, for whatever reason. The therapist explained that he would consider her failure to notify him about a missed session to be a potential danger signal warranting his contacting her family.

In the following session (session six), after the therapist judged that the patient understood the conditions of treatment adequately to agree to them, he moved from the process of contracting to initiating the therapy:

THERAPIST: Okay? We have started . . . *(long pause)* What's on your mind? *(Long pause)*

PATIENT: I don't really feel comfortable talking to you.

THERAPIST: How do you understand that? *(Long pause)*

PATIENT: *(Big sigh)* Your pessimistic attitude.

THERAPIST: In what way is that affecting your wishes to talk with me?

PATIENT: In a sense it's like humoring me.

THERAPIST: Like what?

PATIENT: It's like humoring me.

162

THERAPIST: Humoring you?

PATIENT: Uh, hm.

THERAPIST: I don't understand

PATIENT: If you don't think this is going to be successful, why bother? *(Long pause)*

THERAPIST: Are you saying, when you say that I am humoring you, are you saying I'm doing this as a performer without any real conviction about what I am doing?

PATIENT: No.

THERAPIST: How does humor . . . doesn't humoring mean just to keep you going without any real conviction about what I am doing, isn't that . . .

PATIENT: *(Interrupting while he is speaking)* You may have a conviction. What it is I don't know.

THERAPIST: The sense is that I don't because when you say humoring, it's just pretending, isn't it? . . . So I am pretending *(pause)*.

PATIENT: You may have your own convictions.

THERAPIST: *(Pause)* Such as?

PATIENT: I don't know.

THERAPIST: What are your thoughts about that?

PATIENT: I have no idea.

THERAPIST: Well, let me remind you that you don't feel like talking to me because I am pessimistic.

PATIENT: Uh, hm.

THERAPIST: Which means I have an attitude about you.

PATIENT: Uh, hm.

THERAPIST: I have a conviction about you. What's the nature of this conviction? How do you see it? Let me remind you that you called me pessimistic originally. I said that the situation was serious.

PATIENT: Uh, hm.

THERAPIST: Not hopeless, but very serious.

PATIENT: And you did use the word pessimistic.

THERAPIST: What does pessimistic mean to you?

PATIENT: Umm, not hopeful.

THERAPIST: Hopeless?

PATIENT: Not necessarily hopeless.

THERAPIST: And if I were hopeful, what would that mean in terms of my attitude toward you? In other words, what's missing that would be there if I were hopeful?

PATIENT: Probably a sense that I am going somewhere.

THERAPIST: In other words, you would feel that I think you are going somewhere.

PATIENT: No, that I would feel that I was going somewhere.

THERAPIST: If I said that you were doing all right, you would feel that you were going somewhere? My feeling would make you feel that you are going somewhere?

PATIENT: It might not necessarily make me feel that I was going somewhere. It might give me, it might allow me to fight for the opportunity . . . that I would have the opportunity to go somewhere.

THERAPIST: And my not feeling hopeful then does not permit you to have a sense that you have the opportunity of going somewhere, right?

PATIENT: It certainly affects it.

THERAPIST: So, I am really causing you to lose hope.

PATIENT: Uh, hm.

THERAPIST: And I don't really know what is going to happen. Neither you nor I know what the future is going to bring, am I correct?

PATIENT: Uh, hm.

THERAPIST: So, your experience of me is that I, not knowing what is going to happen, am causing you to lose faith. I think that's a rather malignant attitude of mine, isn't it?

PATIENT: Uh, hm.

Comment

The therapist is trying to proceed with the technique of delineating part self- and part object-representations as is recommended in the early phase of therapy with borderline patients (Kernberg, 1989). He is exploring the meaning of the patient's focus on perceiving him as pessimistic, trying to further define the internal other-representation that she is experiencing.

THERAPIST: So I am not really humoring you, but on the contrary, I'm teasing you in a malignant way . . . cutting off your hope.

PATIENT: I don't think that is your intention.

THERAPIST: But that's how you experience it. And I . . .

PATIENT: *(Interrupting)* Not as doing it intentionally.

THERAPIST: Just being unintentionally malignant?

PATIENT: I don't know if malignant is quite the word either.

THERAPIST: Harmful, unintentionally harmful?

PATIENT: Perhaps.

THERAPIST: So how could we understand that, that I'm being unintentionally harmful?

PATIENT: *(Long pause)* I don't know.

THERAPIST: Well, the least you can say is that there is something going on in me beyond my awareness which is harmful to you. There are bad vibes in me operating against you.

PATIENT: Perhaps, perhaps you aren't aware of the effect.

THERAPIST: And now I am aware because you told me, and I have not changed my attitude. I haven't become more optimistic. At first I have unintentional harmfulness in me. Now, it has become intentional; you told me that, and I have not changed my attitude. So, now I am intentionally harmful.

PATIENT: Is that a statement or a question?

THERAPIST: It's a statement of your experience of me.

PATIENT: *(Long pause)* I don't know if that deduction is accurate, that because you are now aware, you are now intentionally harmful.

THERAPIST: I wouldn't make this statement so strong, if it were not that what you are saying fits with other experiences I had with you during our sessions. May I share with you the impression you convey?

PATIENT: Uh, hm.

THERAPIST: This is true for this session but also for earlier sessions we have had. I have a sense that you are looking at me, almost staring at me, with an almost expressionless face, which conveys a controlled, shall I say somewhat defiant and suspicious, attitude. I would sense this when you would look at me from the beginning of the treatment, more as if you were dealing with an enemy, or somebody in an adversarial function . . .

Comment

Here the therapist is adding information from his observation of the patient's nonverbal communications to the verbal data he is referring to in his effort to delineate the other-representation active in the patient.

> PATIENT: *(Interrupting)* It's correct.
>
> THERAPIST: *(Continuing)* . . . like a prosecuting attorney.
>
> PATIENT: *(Sighs)*
>
> THERAPIST: So, your suspicion of my harmfulness fits with this attitude. I have a sense that you see me really as an enemy, to put it very simply, not as somebody who is here to help you, and that your experience of me is confirmed by this general attitude. Everything I am saying is immediately interpreted in that light. You, you look like somebody who has been captured by the enemy.
>
> PATIENT: *(Pause)* So?
>
> THERAPIST: So . . . it could be that you are attributing to me a similar attitude. In other words, that you are seeing in me something that is really trying to control you from the inside. To put it differently, it may be that you are struggling with powerful malignant forces in you which tend to see me as a danger, precisely because I am here to help you. And that you are attributing to me that same hostile attitude toward you.

Comment

The therapist, having proposed what he feels to be the active other-representation in the patient, is moving on to interpret that representation of him as a projection of a part of the patient's inner world—the projection of a force that, he proposes, is not, in fact, coming from him, but that is active in her beyond her awareness. The therapist is proceeding with the following general strategy: 1) experiencing the affective quality of the session; 2) identifying the characteristics of the "actors" as perceived by the patient; 3) naming the role or roles he perceives ("an enemy"); and 4) interpreting the scene unfolding in the session as the external representation of a conflict the patient harbors in the world of her psychic reality.

The patient may have a number of reactions to the interpretation, ranging from acceptance and increased insight to calling on primitive defense mechanisms in order to continue to protect herself from the anxiety associated with awareness of her intense inner fragmentation and conflicts. In our case example, the patient rejects the interpretation and retreats into a silence that the therapist understands as a deviation from the patient role described in the treatment contract.

PATIENT: I think that is a little far-fetched.

THERAPIST: I may be wrong.

PATIENT: I didn't say your attitude towards me is hostile.

THERAPIST: Malignant.

PATIENT: No, that's also an incorrect word.

THERAPIST: Reflecting your sense that I am consciously harmful to you.

PATIENT: No. I said I think that the deduction is not necessarily accurate—that because you might have unintentionally been harmful that now that you are aware of my feelings that you are now intentionally harmful—I don't think that is necessarily an accurate deduction. *(Long pause)* So?

THERAPIST: Yes, let me remind you that you are expected to talk freely about what's on your mind, and you were looking at me intently so I have a sense that there are things going on in your mind that you don't dare to talk about.

PATIENT: No, my question is where do I go from here?

THERAPIST: Are you asking me?

PATIENT: Uh, hm.

THERAPIST: Do you think I have anything to contribute to that question?

PATIENT: I don't think so.

THERAPIST: How could I? I already told you what we are expected to do, so from here we look at what comes to your mind next.

PATIENT: Well, I don't think we have resolved that issue.

THERAPIST: What issue?

PATIENT: About being harmful.

THERAPIST: Let's see. You obviously don't think that what I said helps you to understand your experience of me as harmful.

PATIENT: Correct.

THERAPIST: What are your thoughts about it?

PATIENT: *(Long pause)* I really don't know.

THERAPIST: So you are rejecting what I have to say, but you don't have anything to add to it either?

PATIENT: *(Pause)* I still feel the same way about talking to you or not talking to you.

THERAPIST: It sounds as if you were saying, "I don't want to talk."

PATIENT: Uh, hm.

THERAPIST: So there's one part of you telling you, "Don't talk."

PATIENT: Uh, hm.

THERAPIST: "Don't participate in this psychotherapy." And you are going along with that, which is interesting . . . *(pause)* because it demonstrates my point.

Comment

In this segment of the session, the therapist moves from pointing out the deviation from the contract to including it in his interpretation that the harmful agency the patient is experiencing is a part of herself rather than a part of him. The clear definition of the patient's role in treatment, which the therapist initially presented in the contract setting and has just reviewed in this session, makes it possible to point to the fact of her not wanting to talk at this point as highly significant: Patient and therapist have before them behavior that speaks to another side of the patient than the one that agreed to the conditions of the contract. Insofar as therapy is geared toward elucidating the unknown sides of the patient, the therapist focuses on the part deviating from the contract since it is beginning to emerge as an unclear and powerful aspect of the patient.

PATIENT: Which point?

THERAPIST: That you are attributing to me something harmful to you which you have difficulty recognizing in yourself. There is something harmful to you going on in you and practically controlling you, telling you: "Don't follow the rules of the game . . . don't speak freely . . . stare into his eyes, make a poker face, let him talk, why should you talk?"

PATIENT: Well, it all goes back to your pessimistic attitude. Why should I talk if the chances of the outcome being positive are so slight?

THERAPIST: It's a nice rationalization. If the chances are slight, why not kill yourself immediately?

PATIENT: I know.

THERAPIST: That is precisely the tempting voice of suicide . . . right here in this session. I think we are talking about something very important. I wouldn't be surprised if after this session you will attempt to try to kill yourself . . . because you have just caught the murderer—that part of you which tells you: "Don't cooperate with treatment, be oppositional, be in revolt, stand up to him, and if it's not enough to be silent, kill yourself."

PATIENT: So.

THERAPIST: Does "so" mean that you have thought out every point?

PATIENT: No, I am waiting for you to continue.

THERAPIST: I made my point.

PATIENT: Hm.

THERAPIST: Or shall we say you have made my point *(pause)*. I think that this is a sign of the part of you which is forcing you to remain silent, to be in opposition. It is also making you waste time.

PATIENT: Waste time, how?

THERAPIST: By not talking, by not exploring further issues that are on your mind. And, of course, it's dramatic what is going on here in this session because you accuse me of not being hopeful.

Comment

The therapist makes it clear both that he takes the therapy very seriously (identifying wasting time in therapy as a self-destructive action) and that he understands the interactions within the session to be the reproduction within a contained environment of the patient's intense intrapsychic forces ("It's dramatic what is going on here in this session").

PATIENT: It's not an accusation. I think it's . . .

THERAPIST: *(Interrupting)* A statement that I'm not hopeful, as if I were not enough on the side of life. When, in fact, I'm here because I am willing to help you.

PATIENT: *(Interrupting)* Right.

THERAPIST: While, while you are doing all you can to defeat your own efforts of treatment. Wasting your time . . .

PATIENT: *(Interrupting)* That goes back to one of my first two questions, which is, Why are you anxious to help me?

THERAPIST: The fact that I am willing to help you is a given: I'm here.

PATIENT: Uh, hm.

THERAPIST: The why is not your problem. What is your problem is your effort to undermine your own and my efforts to work together. That's the issue.

PATIENT: But given the fact that you think that the chances that the outcome will be positive are slight, going back to another question, Why should I then participate?

THERAPIST: Because it may be that the part of you that wants to help yourself, that wants to get better, to live rather than to kill yourself, can work in this therapy. You follow me?

PATIENT: Uh, hm.

THERAPIST: Assuming there is such a part. And I would be willing to assume that, be willing to give it a try. We are testing this at this very moment.

Comment

The therapist emphasizes that what is going on at this moment in therapy is no less real or less critical than anything that goes on in the patient's life outside of therapy. This session ends with the patient challenging the idea that it is the part of her that wants to die that is responsible for her hesitancy to participate fully in the therapy and returning to her idea that it is the therapist's "pessimism" that is causing her to turn away from the treatment. The therapist attempts again to center this pessimism in the patient by referring to the here-and-now of the session:

THERAPIST: . . . the part of you that wants to stop the treatment and kill yourself could have started acting. Yet you have not, in spite of your obvious distrust of me. You are trying to make an effort.

Perhaps part of you is asking yourself, "Maybe this is worthwhile to try?" The major part of you is saying it's not worthwhile to try, it's "pessimistic"—the part of you that wants you to die. You are attributing to me a pessimism that is active in you, at this very moment.

PATIENT: I don't think I'm attributing to you something that's within me. It's a statement that you made, that you were pessimistic.

THERAPIST: I'm talking about your attitude in this session.

PATIENT: Uh, hm.

THERAPIST: And my attitude in this session.

PATIENT: I understand your attitude in this session is pessimistic.

THERAPIST: So you or something in you is ignoring totally my attitude—while at the same time imposing "pessimism" in the sense of "this is worthless, why try?" and moreover keeping you actively antagonistic towards me.

PATIENT: I didn't say your attitude in this particular session is pessimistic. I said your overall attitude is pessimistic and that is a statement that you made.

THERAPIST: *(Pause)* And that you are using conveniently to justify stopping the treatment and perhaps killing yourself.

PATIENT: I'm not using it to justify it.

THERAPIST: That remains to be seen. . . . If this behavior in you is a result of something I said, you can explore the reaction to what I said here and try to understand your reaction.

Comment

This session demonstrates a pattern of therapist interventions that will be repeated again and again in the treatment. In delineating this pattern, we are underlining the importance of referring back to the treatment contract. After the therapist has developed a hypothesis about a specific other-representation he feels is being projected on him by the patient, he describes this "other" in a vivid characterization (a "pessimist with a malignant attitude . . . intentionally harmful . . . an enemy . . . a prosecuting attorney"). The therapist then explains to the patient both that this "other" is actually a part of herself that she is not currently experiencing as such and that this dislocation is leading to a conflict in the session that is an enactment of her intrapsychic conflict. If the patient rejects this interpretation, the therapist points to additional data from the session to support it; these data often include references to the patient's deviating from the conditions of the treatment contract—evidence that different aspects of her inner world are influencing her participation in the session.

We will further illustrate this pattern of therapist intervention with examples from other sessions. Readers reviewing this material may be struck by the similarity of the issues and patterns of conflict that emerge in the sessions even over a long period of time. The material presented from this case may even seem static and boring compared with the drama and turbulence so often encountered in the psychotherapy of borderline patients. Of course, this relative lack of "excitement" is very much the point of setting up a clear treatment contract and frame. While the issues and affects involved in the treatment are, in fact, no less intense or charged than expected in the treatment of a borderline patient, the "microscopic" focus on the interaction within the frame of therapy allows the unfolding of the patient's intrapsychic dynamics in the contained, relatively safe "bonsai" form discussed in chapter 2.

The practice of psychodynamic psychotherapy requires careful attention to both micro and macro levels of analysis. Therapists often err on the side of the former, paying careful attention to the last thing the patient has said, at the expense of gaining an overview of the direction the interaction between patient and therapist—that is, the therapy—is taking. Therapists who have internalized a clear sense of the parameters of the treatment and who regularly ask themselves, "How is this treatment going in relation to the methods and goals we have defined?" are less likely to lose the forest for the trees. In the case we are reviewing, the next ten sessions focus mostly on the patient's not speaking freely enough to satisfy the expectations of the contract. Therapists without a firm belief that the parameters of treatment they have defined are essential for the therapy might step back from this issue and let the patient set the pace here. In this case, however, the therapist works with the conviction that if the patient is not freely reporting what is on her mind, then the therapy cannot happen. He focuses on this point again and again, reminding the patient of the treatment contract and the reasons for it.

In session seven, which follows the session just discussed, the patient begins by asking the therapist if he received a message she had left for him. He responds that he received the message and invites the patient to elaborate on it. She says she doesn't feel like talking about it and assumes a position of silence broken only by terse, laconic comments. The following remarks exemplify the therapist's interventions in this session:

> I'm reviewing the information you have given me about your previous psychotherapy in the light of this session, and it strikes me all of a sudden that you have told me that the same things were going on with Dr. Gray in your previous therapy. You mentioned to me that you used to call him at night or on the weekend so often that he finally couldn't take it. He told you that if you continued calling he would stop the treatment and, if I remember correctly, the immediate reason he stopped the treatment was that you continued to call him anytime, day or night, while at the same time, if I'm correct, fighting him off in the sessions. So I now wonder to what extent the crazy part of you was setting that up—to get him to feel fed up with you and throw you out—in the same way I suggested earlier that the same part of you is trying to provoke me into some kind of retaliatory action here in this session. *(Pause)* I mentioned last time that it was as if everything was in this room— all the aspects of your personality that are connected with your suicide attempts. I would add to this that it is as if the entire treatment with Dr. Gray were being replayed at an accelerated pace here in this session. If I'm correct in what I'm saying, then there exists the urgent possibility of your stopping your treatment.

Comment

In this intervention the therapist is further elaborating his attention to the patient's deviations from the contract. In addition to focusing on her silence, in which she persists in opposition to the general expectations that apply to all patients, he is thinking in terms of the specific threats to the treatment her history reveals. By quickly recognizing the repetition of the pattern of behavior that led to the end of her previous therapy, the therapist intervenes in a way that may lead to insight and make it less likely for her to repeat that pattern. He alludes to the fact

173

that the careful framing of this treatment has led to a quick focus on this pattern ("as if the entire treatment with Dr. Gray were being replayed at an accelerated pace here"), which gradually infiltrated and eventually destroyed her prior treatment. By achieving this focus early in treatment, the therapist makes it clear that repetition of this behavior is incompatible with this treatment. It is no surprise that even though the therapist has already taken this position in the contract-setting sessions, he has to repeat himself here. Patients often hear and agree to conditions of treatment only to continue engaging in behaviors counter to the agreement. Hence the establishment of the treatment contract is only the beginning of the focus on it in therapy. The effectiveness, and even the continued viability, of the therapy may hinge on how the therapist pursues the contract.

The therapist in this example has shown that he is aware of the threat to the treatment and that he will not collude in a pattern of behavior that endangers the treatment. He is attempting to make the patient aware of the aggression and self-destructiveness that are subtending her behavior in the therapy. The therapist is also aware, however, that his interpretation of her indirect attack on the treatment could lead to more direct destructiveness in the form of her simply stopping therapy. There is always the risk that interpretation of the patient's attempts to externalize inner conflicts will lead to flight as the final attempt to avoid facing and experiencing the inner conflicts. For this reason, the therapist predicts this reaction, so that the patient will at least be unlikely to flee treatment ignorant of her motivations for doing so.

This therapist's interventions have been active and appropriate. Nonetheless, the patient maintains a withdrawn position, keeping her thoughts mostly to herself throughout this and the following session. It is important to emphasize the need for careful pursuit of priority issues* in therapy, no matter how much time is required. Many trainee therapists report to supervisors that they "tried that," and since the patient did not respond, they abandoned the issue or approach. The skilled therapist, who will keep returning to the same issue if it is essential to carrying out the treatment, understands that abandoning the issue is

---

*Priority issues include any threat to the treatment discussed in the contract or discovered subsequently and also the issues in the hierarchy of thematic priority presented in chapter 4 of *Psychodynamic Psychotherapy of Borderline Patients* (Kernberg et al., 1989.)

tantamount to giving up on exploratory therapy at that point. In pursuing the essential issue (in this case the patient's silence), the therapist continues to look for data to support his interpretation of the events. Those data may often be gained by observation of the patient's nonverbal channel of communication.

This therapist starts session nine in the following way:

THERAPIST: What's on your mind?

PATIENT: Nothing.

THERAPIST: I can't quite believe that. First of all, because it is almost impossible that nothing should come to one's mind within an extended period of time . . . any period of time beyond a few seconds. Second, because I have a sense your smile indicates that while you are saying "nothing," you're not taking that response very seriously. So it seems to me reasonable to assume that you are not telling me what's on your mind. And if I am correct in assuming that, then the next question is what are the reasons for it. And of course the most obvious reason, the first reason to think of, is that you are afraid to say what's on your mind. But you don't look afraid. And the next most obvious reason, in the light particularly of everything that we have talked about so far, is that it's a compromise solution between a wish to be in treatment and a wish to defeat it. You're coming to these sessions regularly, punctually; you stay through them, which I take as an indication that part of you really would like to be in psychotherapy and get help with your difficulties . . . let's say the healthy part of you . . . the part of you that is concerned, troubled, having difficulties. But another part of you acts as if your main objective would be to defeat this purpose, and I think your silence expresses a submission to that part of you.

Comment

In trying to understand this case, the therapist repeatedly refers the patient's communications, verbal and nonverbal, back to the parameters established in the contract. He takes note of the patient's compliance with the expectations around attendance and points out the significance of that as evidence for a "healthy" part of the patient that wants to work with the therapist to gain ascendance over the aggressive, self-destructive side. The therapist has thus begun to create an image of both the healthy and the destructive sides by relating her compliance/noncompliance to different aspects of the contract.

Session nine provides further illustration of how the therapist refers back to and follows up on the contract. Shortly before the end of the session, the patient states that she will not be able to come at one of the scheduled times and is undecided about whether she will come at an alternate time the therapist offers. The agreement in the treatment contract concerning attendance included a commitment to twice-a-week sessions. If the patient knew in advance that she could not attend a scheduled session, the therapist would offer any possible alternate times in an effort to facilitate attendance. In this session, it may be that the therapist's mention of the patient's regular and punctual attendance earlier has catalyzed the patient's self-destructive side to move in on that front. Faced with this first challenge to the parameter of twice weekly attendance, the therapist elaborates on the contract to make his position on this issue clear:

> THERAPIST: I think what you are initiating is a discussion of whether you want to continue your psychotherapy with me, and therefore I think I should tell you at least in the few minutes that we have left what my action would be in case you stopped coming. I heard from you that you won't show up on Monday, so I'll expect you at the alternate time I proposed on Tuesday. If you don't show up on Tuesday, I would then assume that either you have decided not to continue coming or that you may have made a severe suicide attempt or be dead, and therefore, if you don't show up on Tuesday, I would get in touch with your parents and let them know that you have not shown up for two sessions in a row.
>
> PATIENT: Monday is not a session . . . I told you I will not come.
>
> THERAPIST: Yes, as far as the first session is concerned, you told me that you would not come—but you have not done that with regard to the second one. And under these circumstances, if you do not show up at that session, your parents should know that I am not sure whether you are alive or not and that I am not sure whether your treatment with me will continue or not. I would

see that as my responsibility because I couldn't differentiate whether you had simply decided not to come or whether you had made a severe suicide attempt. Again, if you don't come on Monday, I'll assume that it is because you've told me you would not come.

PATIENT: Very good assumption.

THERAPIST: And, under these circumstances, then we'll talk on Tuesday about whether you wish to continue the treatment or not. You're, of course, fully aware that our commitment is for two sessions a week, and I would consider any reduction of the frequency as incompatible with the treatment that I've committed myself to carry out with you.

PATIENT: I can't help it if that's the only time you have.

Comment

The dialogue continues. The patient becomes increasingly angry that the therapist is focusing on the agreement that she come twice a week. The therapist asks again if she will accept the alternate time. The patient remains equivocal.

THERAPIST: Unless you tell me that you will come on Tuesday, I will not keep that hour open for you. You can understand that I also have other patients to whom I have to offer time, so if I don't hear from you now that you're coming on Tuesday, I'll assume that you are not coming then and I will still expect you on Monday in spite of what you have said because . . .

PATIENT: Do not expect me—can you hear me? Do not expect me!

THERAPIST: . . . that is part of our understanding.

PATIENT: Don't expect to get paid for it; I said I am not coming.

THERAPIST: I hear you. Yes, I hear you, and you will be charged for that session. We will have to talk then about what happens to the treatment and the conditions in which you will not be assuming your financial responsibilities. We have to renegotiate our contract if I see you on Tuesday. We will talk about that, and if you don't come on Tuesday, then I will take the actions that I told you I would. I think I owe it to you that you should

177

know what action I might take under conditions in which you would not fulfill the minimum understanding of our contract.

Comment

This segment of the session illustrates the therapist's attentiveness to issues of the frame and treatment contract. As soon as there is evidence that the patient is deviating from one of the parameters, the therapist focuses on that and reminds the patient of what the treatment requires. He does not overlook it or let it slip by, but rather addresses it as a crucial matter. The degree of affect aroused in the patient demonstrates that this issue is a central one.

In this example we see two of the principles underlying good contract setting and reinforcing. First, the therapist is working to define and maintain conditions of treatment in which he can work comfortably enough to maintain neutrality. He cannot leave the Tuesday alternate time open if the patient does not make it clear she will use it because he knows he will have to take care of scheduling other patients. Treating this patient in a special way by saving that time for her in spite of her indecision could lead to complications in his schedule that might make him resent her special needs and demands.

The second principle illustrated here is that the therapist spells out the contingencies that he would follow if the patient did not respect the parameters of the treatment. Here the therapist describes precisely the steps he would take if the patient did not come to the Tuesday session. This is a context-specific version of the general description of contingencies the therapist goes into during the contract-setting phase.

The previous dialogue also provides an example of the common need to return to a contracting phase to address a basic issue that may have been overlooked or inadequately discussed during the initial contracting. Here, when the therapist takes note of an issue that seems not to have been fully discussed and that now may threaten the treatment (that is, not paying for a session that has been billed for), he points out the need for further clarification of the contractual agreement to prevent a misunderstanding of that issue. After leaving this session, the patient called to say she would take the Tuesday time.

The therapist's focus on maintaining the contract in this session catalyzes a degree of affect in the patient that has not emerged previously in therapy. In the following session, the therapist notes this and points out that the patient's reluctance to speak freely in session ceases when she expresses anger and rage. The patient counters that the issue is not her anger but the therapist's "immoral and corrupt" approach to scheduling and charging for sessions; she charges that this amounts to malpractice.

The patient has not, at this point, agreed with any interpretation that the therapist has made, but she is speaking somewhat more freely. It is important to emphasize that the therapist continues to reiterate his message even though he has met with no agreement from the patient and only slight movement in her degree of participation. The therapist continues to focus on her not speaking freely and to interpret this as a manifestation of her self-destructive part. He now expands his description of this self-representation within her to include repeated references to her ability to talk only "in anger and hatred." He picks up on her characterization of him as "corrupt" and "guilty of malpractice" and weaves this into an intervention in which a rigid "malpractice review board" within her condemns him but does not take issue with her wasting her own and the therapist's time, as well as her parents' money.

Once again, the therapist is attempting to show that what has unfolded in the session between the patient and him is a reflection of forces within her. The patient, whose interest has been aroused by this intervention, has increased her participation in sessions but only, as the therapist repeatedly points out, to argue with him. The healthier part of her, seen in her regular and punctual attendance, remains largely mute.

In the following sessions the therapist doggedly pursues the patient's not speaking freely as deviating from the requirements of treatment and threatening its viability. He further develops his interpretation that the patient is acting in accordance with an internal "malpractice review board" that continues to condemn him while it secretly prohibits her from speaking, thus enacting a "slow suicide" within the very context of the therapy. Confronted with her resistance to this interpretation and her argument that he is the harsh and rigid one, the therapist pursues the approach described earlier through the sixteenth session. At that point, given the patient's continued noncompliance with the need to speak freely in treatment, the therapist questions if there is any point in the treatment going on. The session begins with a long silence.

THERAPIST: I think we should talk about what your plans are and whether you are willing to work psychotherapeutically with me or not. You are giving all indications that you are not willing to do that, and I can respect that. The question is whether you have really been thinking about the alternatives, or whether there may be some idea in you that without your assuming your responsibility here anything good could come of this therapy. Should you harbor such an illusion, it could only be damaging to you in terms of playing into your waste of time and money. So I think the time may have come for us to talk about this.

PATIENT: I told you I had a hard time talking.

THERAPIST: At the beginning of this session it didn't look like you were having a hard time talking, but it looked like you were preparing yourself for setting up a demonstrative silence. I am convinced that you're in collusion with whatever makes you remain silent and that the part of you that would be able to do work is totally playing into the hands of the part of you that wants to kill yourself. That may indeed preclude psychotherapy. There is no way around your carrying out your work in this psychotherapy, which is to come into each session and talk about your difficulties. . . . When I talk about your talking about your difficulties, I am not referring to laconic statements, but to an ongoing effort to communicate fully to me everything that is on your mind. If you were *trying* to talk—stuttering, stammering, looking in despair because you are trying to overcome silence and unable to do it—then I might be able to believe that you can't talk.

Comment

The therapist has worked with this patient for a number of weeks on the same issue—her holding back in session. Initially he points out to her that this, combined with calling between sessions, is what led to the end of her prior therapy. He goes on to interpret the splitting and projections he perceives, developing the image of the internal "malpractice review board" that allows her to speak only in angry accusations about his unfairness as it proceeds to carry out a "slow suicide."

After working along these lines for ten sessions—after taking the time to see what understanding he can arrive at concerning her behavior and what impact his interventions might have—with minimal progress in terms of the patient speaking freely, the therapist has come to the clinical judgment that the therapy may, in fact, not be viable. He presents this to the patient, referring to the same principles as in the contract setting: "There is no way around your carrying out your work in this psychotherapy." His intervention is different from the contract setting insofar as he is not simply stating what the treatment requires, but is suggesting an interpretation of the patient's not complying with those requirements. The therapist's comments here also address the patient's unflagging wish for magic, for an omnipotent other: ". . . some idea in you that even without your assuming your responsibility here something good may come of it."

There is no guarantee that confronting the patient's noncompliance will lead to change in her behavior. Many similar cases might end at this point. In this case, however, the patient's response was to begin to participate more freely in the session. A therapist's statement of concern that a therapy is not viable may be the intervention that leads to change in the patient; yet patients and skeptical therapists often charge that such a statement is a "threat." It is important to keep in mind that the primary reason for this kind of statement is sincere doubt that the therapy can be carried out and an accompanying readiness to end the treatment if indicated; the only threat is the threat that the patient's behavior poses to the treatment.

It is naive to think that change in the course of a therapy will be effected once and for all, without regression. In the case under discussion, although the patient responded to the therapist's setting this limit regarding her not speaking freely, the issue re-emerges further on in the treatment, as a session at the nine-month point shows:

THERAPIST: I have a sense that in what you're telling me—you remember what I said on Tuesday—that you're leaving out something very important. So I didn't just say that you're afraid to tell me about yourself.

PATIENT: I know.

THERAPIST: Well, what else did I say? What reason did I suggest might exist for not sharing with me what's on your mind or not talking about yourself during the session . . . and, to the contrary, trying to kill time during the session? I made a hypothesis about what might motivate you to behave that way. . . . It's what I have given most emphasis to and I think that this forgetting may be significant itself. . . . I said that you were behaving this way because you were submitting to one part of you that is set to destroy your treatment and to destroy your life—a sadistic, cruel, self-destructive but very powerful and self-righteous enemy sitting inside of you.

Comment

This sounds familiar. It reminds us of how persistent and repetitive the therapist must be. The effect of this careful technique is to maintain the holding environment of therapy in an effort to facilitate gradual change in the patient. Later in this session:

> PATIENT: I know there's a lot of things that are on my mind *(pause)*. I think ever since the time I was first in therapy I wanted to discuss what happened to me *(pause)*. Yes, a number of things were happening when I was crying out; I guess I was embarrassed they were happening.

Comment

There is a different quality here to the patient's participation. She is gradually speaking more openly, and with more ability to observe herself in the process. Her work in therapy increases, accompanied by changes in her life over time. And yet, we find in a session two years into treatment:

> THERAPIST: *(After a long pause)* Apparently I'll have to remind you what the nature of our work in this session is.
> PATIENT: In this particular one or any one?
> THERAPIST: In this or in any.
> PATIENT: *(Pause)* Happy New Year! *(Pause)* No comment? Or don't you know what I'm referring to there either? Do you think I'm just coming out with these bizarre comments today? *(Pause)* We began therapy exactly two years ago . . . it's the beginning of the third year.

THERAPIST: I thought this silence to be one with a meaning. What do you want to say?

PATIENT: No comment?

THERAPIST: No, I'm listening.

PATIENT: I'm asking you. Why are you starting in again?

THERAPIST: Starting what?

PATIENT: I'm asking you a question.

THERAPIST: Yes, but do I need to repeat what the nature of our work is?

PATIENT: So, I'm not allowed to ask you a question?

THERAPIST: Oh, yes. You're allowed to ask me questions, but I may not necessarily answer all your questions.

PATIENT: I'm asking you a question.

THERAPIST: Well, I guess I have to remind you that the nature of our work together consists of your saying freely what comes to mind and my commenting on it when I feel I have something to contribute. Sometimes what comes to your mind may come in the form of a question. I may or may not answer, according to what I feel is most useful.

PATIENT: According to your whim?

THERAPIST: According to my understanding or lack of understanding and my sense of what I may have to contribute.

Comment

Two years into the treatment the therapist does not hesitate to review a part of the contract, almost verbatim. The patient's insistence that he answer a question, while interesting in itself, is not in accord with the patient and therapist roles as initially defined. In an attempt to help the patient step back from her position that the therapist answer her and think about what her insistence may represent, the therapist carefully reviews the relevant part of the contract. While this degree of resistance in the patient at the two-year point may at first seem disheartening, it is important to note two things. First, overall, the patient has moved beyond her noncompliance with speaking freely and is now participating in a way that brings up further material. Second, the contract, and its immediate relevance to each session, will continue to be an important reference point until the therapy has been completed.

CHAPTER 8

Research Involving the Treatment Contract

IN THIS FINAL CHAPTER we introduce our clinical research ideas, hypotheses, and results to date as they relate to the clinical significance of the therapeutic contract with the borderline patient. From the start, our primary interest has been to explore the clinical complexities involved in treating this patient population, which has traditionally presented a challenge to therapists.

In the interest of clinical research, there is good reason to focus on the initial contract-setting period in the psychotherapy of borderline patients. Borderline personality disorder (BPD) patients often approach treatment with a new therapist in a state of crisis. The crisis can have a precipitating stress (for example, loss or threatened loss of an intimate other) or be one in which the patient is demanding immediate and magical relief for symptoms in the form of the therapist's total availability and/or a substitute such as medication. Treatment is often conceived of, or treated as, a magical solution, something that will be done to and for the patient with absolute results.

The way the patient is introduced to treatment is probably predictive of the course of the treatment. Done well, the contract period leads the patient into therapy with realistic expectations and with structures

184

in place that will allow treatment to occur despite the difficult characteristics of the pathology. Done poorly, the early phase of treatment can contribute to premature termination of treatment, or treatment that is flawed and unproductive. We set out to study these ideas as rigorously as the current state of psychotherapy research would allow.

The Dropout Problem

One consideration that initiated our desire to study the treatment contract was the hypothesis that it was related to the issue of the high dropout rate of the borderline patient. In any psychotherapy study, a high patient dropout rate creates difficulties. From a design and statistical analysis point of view, dropouts destroy the randomization procedure. The dropout rate also raises questions about the generalizability of the treatment results obtained from the patients who remain in therapy. From a treatment point of view, the patients who drop out are not profiting from the therapy, and one wonders how the treatment itself can be improved in order to reach these patients.

The high dropout rate typical in the treatment of borderline patients is hardly surprising when one reviews the criteria for this Axis-II disorder. The borderline patient is unstable in interpersonal relations—a phenomenon likely to be repeated with the therapist. She is often angry and is labile in mood. She is prone to act on feelings rather than to explore them (the goal of the therapy) and tends to discharge them through impulsive action (whether it be in the form of sexual acting out, eating problems, or other self-destructive behavior).

Robert Waldinger and John Gunderson (1984) surveyed eleven clinicians who were particularly experienced in the treatment of borderline patients. These therapists were asked to report on their treatment (psychoanalysis or intensive psychotherapy) of patients with either DSM-III BPD or borderline personality organization. Forty-six percent of the patients dropped out within the first six months of treatment. Of all the premature terminations, 44 percent were judged by therapists to be precipitous, and 60 percent were against advice. The therapists indicated that 50 percent of the total who terminated prematurely did so because they felt they had achieved sufficient symptom relief and were satisfied with their improvement. Twenty-two percent terminated

185

in the context of a treatment impasse, 5 percent in the face of family opposition to the treatment, and 18 percent because of unavoidable realities, such as job changes or geographic moves.

Andrew Skodol and colleagues (1983) compared the dropout rates of borderline, neurotic, other personality disordered patients and of schizophrenic patients treated in an outpatient clinic. BPD patients demonstrated the highest dropout rate. Sixty-seven percent of BPD patients accepted for treatment dropped out within three months, while 38 percent of the neurotic or other personality disorder group and only 14 percent of the schizophrenic group terminated within the same time period.

Gunderson and co-workers (1989) reported on a prospective study of psychotherapy discontinuation among sixty borderline patients whose treatment began in a hospital setting. Patients were discharged from the hospital to continue psychotherapy as outpatients when clinically indicated. Of the entire sample, 43 percent had dropped out of psychotherapy within six months. A substantial fraction of the initial cohort remained in the hospital for the full duration of the dropout study. Since it is likely that milieu factors in the hospital tended to discourage these patients' ending treatment, their reported dropout rate may be deceptively low. When only those patients who entered outpatient treatment at some point during the six months were included, 66 percent had dropped out by the six-month point.

In contrast to these dropout rates, one must consider the research conducted by Linehan. Sixteen percent of twenty-two patients dropped out during the first year of treatment (Linehan, personal communication). Two of these patients dropped out during the initial four weeks of treatment (the induction phase), and the other two dropped out later on in the treatment. One way to understand Linehan's lower dropout rate is that she provides a supportive treatment that may encourage patients to stay in therapy. To date, we have not distinguished in research studies between patients needing supportive psychodynamic therapy versus expressive dynamic therapy. Nor have we included in our research design the assistance of a social worker whose help may be indicated for some patients to structure their lives and deal with external stresses. Linehan's treatment provides patients with more treatment contact per week: two individual sessions, group therapy, and phone contact at the patient's discretion.

In summary, some studies find that the dropout rate for BPD patients is twice the rate for those with neurotic and other personality disorders, and four times the rate for schizophrenics, with only 33 percent of the borderline patients remaining in the treatment at the three-month point (Skodol et al., 1983). Other studies show that by six months of treatment, only from 34 percent to 57 percent of BPD outpatients remain in therapy (Gunderson et al., 1989; Waldinger & Gunderson, 1984).

CLINICAL FACTORS RELATED TO THE DROPOUT PROBLEM

Our point of view is not, however, to consider the BPD patient as an isolated individual who either remains in or prematurely ends treatment. Therapy is a process between two people, and the specific patient-therapist relationship is crucial. In this chapter, we will examine aspects of both patient and therapist contribution to premature dropout with the practical aim of finding answers to two questions: What are the initial threats to continuation in treatment? and How can the treatment approach be modified to support treatment continuation?

Our basic operating hypothesis is that ultimately it is the interaction at a specific point in the treatment history between a particular borderline patient, with her unique combination of pathology and assets, and a particular therapist that determines continuation or dropout. If we can explain the nature of successful therapeutic interactions, we can be more specific in teaching therapists the most relevant variables to attend to and the most efficacious interventions.

The data for this analysis come from our study of the psychodynamic psychotherapy of borderline patients (Clarkin, Koenigsberg, et al., 1992). To date, thirty-four female borderline patients have been carefully diagnosed and assigned to outpatient psychodynamic psychotherapy. Patient and therapist meet for two sessions each week, and the therapy is expected to last approximately two years. The therapists are psychiatrists and psychologists, some still in advanced training, who have been instructed in this form of treatment (Kernberg et al., 1989). In addition, a senior clinician supervises each therapist. Audio- and video-tapes of the sessions are used to verify the therapists' adherence to and skill in delivering the treatment. Periodic assessments of the patients are made to note progress in terms of symptoms, social functioning, and changes in borderline pathology.

We chose the contract-setting process and the therapeutic alliance as variables that likely correlate with whether a patient remains in therapy or drops out. The potential relevance of the contract setting to dropout rates emerged in an early review of the cases in our psychotherapy research project. A number of therapists did not adhere closely to the instructions of the therapy manual in setting up the treatment contract (for example, the two cases discussed in chapter 6). These cases tended to end in dropout. We developed a rating scale (see the appendix) to apply to the contract-setting process in order to study the hypothesis that inadequate handling of the contracting phase of therapy correlated with a high dropout rate.

Our interest in the therapeutic alliance stemmed from the fact that the alliance is one of the few therapy variables that has been shown to correlate with outcome (Orlinsky & Howard, 1986). Because of the problems involved in conceptualizing and fostering the therapeutic alliance with borderline patients, who often experience strong negative transference in therapy, it seemed logical to investigate the correlation between the alliance and the dropout rate in this population. It also seemed that the therapeutic alliance could be understood as flowing out of the treatment contract since the alliance is the putting-into-action of the model of therapy described in the contract. From a different angle, the contract could be viewed as a sort of exoskeleton, in which the alliance can emerge and in which the treatment can be contained during those periods when stormy transference (and countertransference) may threaten the alliance.

Research Procedures

From a research as well as a clinical point of view, the contract-setting period in dynamic treatment offers an excellent opportunity to gather data on the patient, the therapist, and the unique interaction between the two individuals. The contract-setting period is a time in the therapy when the therapist introduces standardized (by the treatment manual) stimuli into the interaction, and the patient is given an opportunity to respond to these stimuli (that is, the description of therapist and patient responsibilities during the treatment). Since the therapist's behavior is relatively standardized by the treatment manual, one can rate the patient's response to the therapist's behavior as one would rate a response to a standardized test (for example, the Rorschach or the Thematic Apperception Test). We have gone yet a step further, and have rated the therapist's response to the patient's response. This is, of course, a rating of the adequacy of the therapist's pursuit of difficulties and resistance raised by the patient.

Without going into technical detail that can best be obtained elsewhere (Yeomans et al., forthcoming), we will briefly describe the instruments that we used to examine patient characteristics and patient-therapist interaction as they relate to dropout rates.

INSTRUMENTS

The two basic instruments we employed in the investigation of the therapeutic alliance and the contract-setting period in the treatment of borderline patients were our own Contract Rating Scale (CRS) and the California Psychotherapy Alliance Scales-Rater Version (CALPAS-R).

The CRS was devised by the present authors in order to rate reliably the contract-setting process in the dynamic treatment of borderline patients as defined by Kernberg and colleagues (1989). The unit of rating is the whole contract-setting phase of therapy, usually two or more transcribed sessions. The CRS has four components: 1) the therapist's presentation of the conditions of treatment (statement of the treatment contract); 2) the patient's response to these conditions; 3) the therapist's pursuit of the patient's response/resistance; and 4) the degree of consensus. The CALPAS-R (Marmar & Gaston, 1989; Marmar et al., 1986) is composed of four dimensions: 1) patient working capacity (both positive and negative contributions); 2) patient commitment; 3) working strategy consensus; and 4) therapist understanding and involvement.

To obtain more information about factors related to the dropout problem, we also devised a semistructured interview guide a researcher could use in a telephone interview with a patient about her experience in either continuing or dropping out of our psychodynamic treatment. The guide (with some standard probing questions) was of assistance to the interviewer in assuring coverage of key areas and uniformity of data across subjects.

Dropout Rate and Patient Characteristics

To date, we have evaluated and begun outpatient treatment with thirty-four female BPD patients. There have been seven patients (21 percent) who ended treatment prior to or during the treatment contract-setting period. By three months of treatment, five additional patients had dropped out prematurely, yielding a cumulative 35 percent dropout rate by that time. This dropout rate is comparable to that reported by others. Our 35 percent dropout rate at twelve weeks compares favorably to the 67 percent rate reported by Andrew Skodol and colleagues (1983) in their outpatient study, and the 48 percent rate reported by Solomon Goldberg and colleagues (1986) in their outpatient medication study.

We believe that our dropout rate was affected by a number of treatment variables. First of all, while we are developing an instrument to assess adherence to the treatment manual, and have developed a reliable instrument to do so, we are not yet doing these assessments "on line" (simultaneous with the conducting of the therapy) so as to ensure adherence to the manual of on-going cases. Second, for pragmatic and investigatory reasons, the study includes both experienced and inexperienced therapists in this pilot stage. The experienced therapists have a different dropout rate (or curve) than the inexperienced therapists. The patients working with experienced therapists are less likely to drop out, and if they do drop out, it is later than with inexperienced therapists.

A clinical factor that likely affects our dropout rate is that the borderline patients in our study tend to be very disturbed. The majority of our patients have a significant history of most, if not all, of the eight BPD criteria, and many have been nonfunctional and have histories of multiple hospitalizations. Many of these patients entered our psychotherapy project directly from an inpatient treatment required to address significant depressive, suicidal, and/or self-destructive behavior.

Thus our dropout rate may be related to the severity of pathology of the BPD patients, the range of experience of the therapists, and the lack of ongoing monitoring of their adherence to a complex manual. On the other hand, the pilot phase during which these variables were not carefully controlled provides us with some information relevant to the dropout phenomenon.

We will first consider some patient characteristics—pathology, strengths, withholding behavior in therapy—as potentially related to dropout.

PATIENT PATHOLOGY

One hypothesis is that the severity of the borderline pathology in a given patient, or the severity of certain aspects of borderline pathology (for example, one or more key criteria), is related to the likelihood of premature termination from therapy. To explore this hypothesis, we have devised a rating scale to measure the severity of each of the eight BPD criteria in Axis II. This scale is anchored so that scores of 1 and 2 are subthreshold for the criterion, a score of 3 is the criterion as stated in DSM-III-R, Axis II, and scores of 4 through 6 are more severe.

Using the dimensional scores of the BPD criteria, we have factor analyzed the eight criteria with a large number of BPD patients (N = 76) (Clarkin et al., forthcoming). Three factors emerge: 1) an identity diffusion factor composed of the identity diffusion, emptiness/boredom, fear of abandonment, and unstable relations criteria; 2) an affective factor composed of labile moods, anger, and suicidal and self-destructive behavior; and 3) an impulsive behavior factor composed of the criterion requiring impulsivity in at least two areas.

We used both the total BPD score (ranging from 15 to 48) and the scores on each of the three BPD factors to see if we could distinguish the early dropout patients from those patients who remained in treatment. To our surprise, there was no difference between the two groups.

While degree of borderline pathology does not distinguish these groups (possibly because of the restricted range of borderline pathology needed to meet the DSM-III-R diagnosis), we looked at another aspect of pathology: daily functioning. The daily routine and structure of the patient's life may be an important factor in treatment continuation.

To explore the experience of patients who dropped out as compared to that of those who remained in treatment, we contacted the first eighteen patients admitted to the study some six months to one year after initiation of treatment. Using a standardized format, we interviewed patients on the telephone for approximately thirty minutes each.

We examined eleven patients who dropped out prematurely and seven patients who continued in treatment for over one year. Six of the seven "remainers" were either full-time students or working, while only two of five early dropouts and two of four late dropouts (overall, four of the nine dropouts who responded to this question) were working. It would appear that patients who stay in treatment are more likely to be engaged in productive activity that gives their lives a schedule, or routine. This may be tantamount to saying that the most functional patients are also most functional in their treatment, or it may be saying that having a daily or weekly schedule is an important adjunct to this treatment.

PATIENT STRENGTHS

While the general level of borderline pathology (1 to 6 rating of each of the eight criteria) does not distinguish dropouts from remainers, it is quite plausible that certain patient strengths would be important factors in continuing treatment. It may well be that personality characteristics other than those related to the borderline pathology are most predictive of engagement in therapy. We are only beginning to gather data on this issue.

Our clinical sense is that patient assets are important, not only in the initial engagement phase but in response to the treatment throughout. This is not an original observation, and Michael Stone (1990), for one, has noted in his follow-up study that borderline patients with certain characteristics, such as obsessiveness, have a better course.

One of our most successfully treated cases was that of A.B., a twenty-eight-year-old single female with a history of multiple hospitalizations and ruptured treatments. In order to capture some of her personality strengths as well as weaknesses, we administered the NEO personality inventory (NEO-PI; Costa & McCrae, 1985). The instrument measures five traits that have shown up in personality research for years, including neuroticism, extroversion, openness, agreeableness, and conscientiousness. Her NEO-PI profile is characterized by an average level of neuroticism, agreeableness, and conscientiousness, and she scored very high on the extroversion and openness scales. This is in contrast to the average scores for a borderline sample of fifteen other patients in which neuroticism is in the very high range and both agreeableness and conscientiousness are in the low range. In contrast to the larger BPD group, therefore, A.B. shows many more strengths, with only an average neuroticism score, and average scores for trust (in the agreeableness trait) and ability to adhere to a project once begun (conscientiousness). The high openness scale suggests a willingness to share conflicted feelings with a therapist.

An important element that has not often been mentioned in the literature is the time in the life of the patient (or point in the history of the illness) at which the treatment episode occurs. It has been our impression that those patients who have failed in previous treatment contacts, and who have "hit bottom," are those most likely to engage in treatment.

PATIENT WITHOLDING

Two findings related to dropout emerged from our telephone interviews. Of the dropouts, five of ten patients on whom we were able to obtain these data said they did not discuss ending the treatment with their therapists in the last few sessions. Instead, they simply stopped showing up for the sessions. The five who did not discuss termination included all four of the early dropouts and one of the late dropouts. In summary, none of the early dropouts discussed the termination while the majority of late dropouts (six of seven) did. This has several implications. First of all, therapists should be alert to any material suggesting thoughts about dropping out, even though these thoughts may not be explicitly verbalized. The patient has a better chance of keeping her thoughts from becoming actions if they are verbalized and discussed with the therapist. Second, the treatment contract is not a once-and-for-all agreement, but rather a very tentative working contract that must be repeatedly referred to, reintroduced, and renegotiated (see chapter 7).

The second finding was the interesting discovery that the seven patients who remained in therapy perceived the structure of the treatment (that is, contract setting, limit setting, and so on) as helpful and supportive in their attempts to introduce organization into their chaotic lives. This finding is especially striking in light of the fact that virtually all patients who started the treatment had objections to the contract when it was initially discussed.

THERAPIST-PATIENT INTERACTION

Contract rating and CALPAS

To date we have rated sixteen of our cases with the CALPAS-R and eighteen on the CRS. We examined the relationship of these ratings to each other and to treatment remainer/dropout status.

There were two significant correlations between the two instruments. The negative Patient Working Capacity on the CALPAS and the Patient Contribution on the CRS showed a significant negative correlation ($r = -.64$; $p = .01$). That is, as the negative Patient Working Capacity on the CALPAS became more pronounced, the positive Patient Contribution to the contract-setting process went down. The correlation between the CALPAS Therapist Understanding and Involvement (TUI) and the Consensus Rating on the CRS was positive and significant ($r = .52$; $p = .05$). The correlation between the TUI on the CALPAS and the Total Score on the CRS approached significance ($r = .49$; $p = .07$). From a content point of view, since these relationships would be expected, they raise our confidence in the scales themselves.

We then examined the relationship between the therapeutic alliance and quality of contract setting and the length of time the patient stayed in treatment. We assumed that there would be a positive relationship among relatively good therapeutic alliance, adequate contract setting, and continuation in treatment. The number of sessions a patient stayed in treatment ranged from a low of 7 to a high of 455 in our sample. Since the distribution was skewed, we normalized it by a log transformation.

First, the correlation between the CALPAS Therapist Understanding and Involvement subscore and the number of sessions was $r = .64$; $p = .007$. The correlation between the Therapist Contribution subscale of the CRS (which includes the therapist's presentation of the contract and pursuit of the patient's response) and the number of sessions was $r = .50$; $p = .04$. Likewise, the correlation between the total score on the CRS and number of sessions was $r = .50$; $p = .04$.

These data, while tentative because of the small sample, suggest a direction that is helpful in our standardization of a treatment. It would appear that the therapist's technique and skills are more critical than the patient's level of pathology. Severity of borderline pathology did not correlate with dropout, but the therapist's contribution to the therapeutic alliance and to the contract setting did. An alternative explanation would be that, due to our research procedures, we selected more homogeneous patients and more heterogeneous therapists. Our patients are not a heterogeneous group of BPD patients, but a relatively sick or seriously disturbed group, at least on the eight criteria of DSM-III-R.

Implications

The dropout problem is understandable with borderline patients, whose pathology tends toward difficulties in collaboration, flight from exploratory work, and defenses against integration and change.

The data reported here suggest that the therapist's contribution to the contract-setting process and to the overall therapeutic alliance is an important element in the successful induction of the borderline patient into treatment. We must begin to describe in more specific ways the interventions of the successful therapist with the BPD patient. What do therapists who have received high ratings for their contribution to the alliance actually do? We suggest that at those moments in treatment that are marked by resistance, the successful therapist:

1. Takes note of the resistance with its related affect and, as seen in chapter 7, refers repeatedly to the initial contract in pointing out and discussing the resistance
2. Explores the resistance
3. Carries out this exploration with equanimity and without hostility
4. In the process of exploration, gives the patient the opportunity to discover issues underlying the resistance
5. If necessary, interprets to the patient why she acted as she did (for example, the therapist might say something like "Since you believed that I was trying to hurt you, it was necessary for you to do that")

The borderline patient resists the treatment, starting with the contract-setting period, in numerous ways. Examples of these challenges and methods of dealing with them have been provided in the previous chapters of this book. Our research to date has focused mostly on the importance of the contract in the induction phase of treatment and in relation to the problem of patients dropping out of therapy, but a well-established contract, internalized by therapist and patient, can also play a critical role in keeping the psychodynamic work on track. The contract helps the therapist maintain a position of neutrality and attend to the analysis of transference and countertransference in treatments where there is often intense pressure to support, counsel, take sides, and accept dependency. Future research should provide further data on this ongoing therapeutic function of the treatment contract.

APPENDIX

Contract Rating Scale

Rater_____

Patient : _____   Session #_____

Therapist: _____

TREATMENT CONTRACT RATING SCALE - I

Patient Responsibilities
-attendance
-fees
-method of treatment

<u>Step 1</u>: Rating the therapist as to how well he has presented the patient's responsibilities in treatment.

Rating

1	2	3	4	5
Poorly				Thoroughly

<u>Step 2</u>: Rating of the patient's response to Step 1 (therapist's presentation): a) degree to which patient heard it

Rating

1	2	3	4	5
Not at all				Fully

b) degree to which patient accepted it

Rating

1	2	3	4	5
Not at all				Fully

Step 3: Rating therapist's reaction to Step 2 (patient's response).

Rating

1	2	3	4	5
Inadequate				Excellent

Step 4: Rating of degree of consensus between patient and therapist regarding patient's understanding of and acceptance of her responsibilities. This is a global rating.

Rating

1	2	3	4	5
None				Full

TREATMENT CONTRACT RATING SCALE - II

Therapist Responsibilities
- attending to the schedule
- making every effort to understand and, when useful, comment
- clarifying the limits of his involvement
- explaining policy of confidentiality (if asked)

Step 1: Rating the therapist as to:
a) how well he has presented his responsibilities;

Rating

1	2	3	4	5
Poorly				Thoroughly

b) how well he delineates the limits of his involvement.

Rating

1	2	3	4	5
Poorly				Thoroughly

Step 2: Rating of the patient's response to Step 1 (therapist's presentation).
a) degree to which patient heard it

Rating

1	2	3	4	5
Not at all				Fully

b) degree to which patient accepted it

Rating

1	2	3	4	5
Not at all				Fully

Step 3: Rating therapist's reaction to Step 2 (patient's response).

Rating

1	2	3	4	5
Inadequate				Excellent

Step 4: Rating of degree of consensus between patient and therapist regarding patient's understanding of and acceptance of therapist's responsibilities. This is a global rating.

Rating

1	2	3	4	5
None				Fully

TREATMENT CONTRACT RATING SCALE - III

Threats to Treatment

Step 1: Rating of how well therapist states the specifics of the treatment contract around the 1 or 2 areas of pathology which he predicts will be most germane to this patient and will pose the greatest threat to treatment. This includes his statement of why he has chosen these areas (i.e., that the prediction is based on what the patient's history and presentation have revealed) and his outline of the steps which the patient will be expected to take in order to deal with the threats to the treatment specific to her case.

Rating

1	2	3	4	5
Inadequate				Adequate

Step 2: Rating of the patient's response to Step 1 (therapist's presentation).

Rating

1	2	3	4	5
Rejecting				Accepting

Step 3: Rating therapist's reaction to Step 2 (patient's response).

Rating

1	2	3	4	5
Inadequate				Excellent

<u>Step 4</u>: Rating of degree of consensus between patient and therapist regarding specific content areas. This is a global rating.

Rating

1	2	3	4	5
None				Full

Content Areas Selected by Therapist	Are content areas chosen by the therapist <u>the</u> crucial ones
1._____	Yes _____ No _____
_____	If no, list ones felt to be crucial _____
2._____	
_____	_____
	_____

References

Bloom, H., and Rosenbluth, M. 1989. The use of contracts in the inpatient treatment of the borderline personality disorder. *Psychiatric Quarterly*, *60*(4), 317–27.

Bordin, E. S. 1979. The generalizability of the psychoanalytic concept of the working alliance. *Psychotherapy: Theory, Research, and Practice*, *16*(3), 252–60.

Buie, D., and Adler, G. 1982. The definitive treatment of the borderline personality. *International Journal of Psychoanalysis and Psychotherapy, 9,* 51–87.

Chessick, R. 1979. A practical approach to the psychotherapy of the borderline patient. *American Journal of Psychotherapy, 33,* 531–46.

Clarkin, J. F., Hull, J. W., and Hurt, S. W. In press. *Factor structure of borderline personality disorder criteria. Journal of Personality Disorders.*

Clarkin, J. F., Koenigsberg, H., Yeomans, F., et al. 1992. Psychodynamic psychotherapy of the borderline patient. In J. F. Clarkin, E. Marziali, and H. Munroe-Blum (Eds.), *Borderline personality disorder: Clinical and empirical perspectives* (pp. 268–87). New York: Guilford.

Costa, P. T., Jr., and McCrae, R. R. 1985. *The NEO personality inventory manual.* Odessa, Fl.: Psychological Assessment Resources.

DEWALD, P. A. 1969. *Psychotherapy: A dynamic approach*, 2nd ed.. New York: Basic Books.

FRANK, A. F., AND GUNDERSON, J. G. 1990. The role of the therapeutic alliance in the treatment of schizophrenia. *Archives of General Psychiatry*, 47, 228–36.

FREUD, S. [1912] 1958. *Recommendations to physicians practising psychoanalysis*. The Standard Edition, Vol. 12 (pp. 109–21). London: Hogarth Press.

FRIESWYK, S. H., COLSON, D. B., AND ALLEN, J. G. 1984. Conceptualizing the therapeutic alliance from a psychoanalytic perspective. *Psychotherapy*, 21, 460–64.

GIOVACCHINI, P. 1979. *Treatment of primitive mental states*. New York: Jason Aronson.

GOLDBERG, S. C., SCHULZ, C., SCHULZ, P. M., ET AL. 1986. Borderline and schizotypal personality disorders treated with low-dose thiothixene vs. placebo. *Archives of General Psychiatry*, 43, 680–86.

GUNDERSON, J. 1984. *Borderline personality disorder*. Washington, D.C.: American Psychiatric Press.

GUNDERSON, J., FRANK, A. F., KATZ, H. M., ET AL. 1984. Effects of psychotherapy in schizophrenia: II. Comparative outcome of two forms of treatment. *Schizophrenia Bulletin*, 10(4), 564–98.

GUNDERSON, J., FRANK, A. F., RONNINGSTAM, E. F., ET AL. 1989. Early discontinuance of borderline patients from psychotherapy. *Journal of Nervous and Mental Disease*, 177(1), 38–42.

HELLMAN, I. D., MORRISON, T. L., AND ABRAMOWITZ, S. I. 1986. The stresses of psychotherapeutic work: A replication and extension. *Journal of Clinical Psychology*, 42, 197–205.

KERNBERG, O. F. 1975. *Borderline conditions and pathological narcissism*. New York: Jason Aronson.

———. 1977. The structural diagnosis of borderline personality organization. In P. Hartocollis (Ed.), *Borderline personality disorders* (pp. 87–121). New York: International Universities Press.

———. 1984. *Severe personality disorders: Psychotherapeutic strategies*. New Haven: Yale University Press.

———. 1989. The narcissistic personality disorder and the differential diagnosis of antisocial behavior. *Psychiatric Clinics of North America*, 12, 553–70.

KERNBERG, O. F., SELZER, M. A., KOENIGSBERG, H. W., ET AL. 1989. *Psychodynamic psychotherapy of borderline patients*. New York: Basic Books.

KLERMAN, G. L., WEISSMAN, M. M., ROUNSAVILLE, B. J., AND CHEVRON, E. S.

1984. *Interpersonal psychotherapy of depression.* New York: Basic Books.

LANGS, R. 1976. *The bipersonal field.* New York: Jason Aronson.

LANGS, R., AND STONE, L. 1980. *The therapeutic experience and its setting: A clinical dialogue.* New York: Jason Aronson.

LAPLANCHE, J., AND PONTALIS, J. B. 1973. *The language of psychoanalysis.* New York: W. W. Norton.

LINEHAN, M. M. IN PRESS. *Dialectical behavior therapy for treatment of parasuicidal women: Treatment manual.*

———. 1987. Dialectical behavior therapy: A cognitive approach to parasuicide. *Journal of Personality Disorders, 1,* 328–33.

LUBORSKY, L. 1984. *Principles of psychoanalytic psychotherapy: A manual for supportive and expressive treatment.* New York: Basic Books.

MALTSBERGER, J. T., AND BUIE, D. H. 1974. Countertransference hate in the treatment of suicidal patients. *Archives of General Psychiatry, 30,* 625–33.

MARMAR, C. R., AND GASTON, L. 1989. *Manual of California Psychotherapy Alliance Scales (CALPAS).* San Francisco: Unpublished manuscript.

MARMAR, C. R., HOROWITZ, M., WEISS, D., AND MARZIALI, E. 1986. The development of the therapeutic alliance rating system. In L. Greenberg and W. Pinsof (Eds.), *The psychotherapeutic process: A research handbook.* New York: Guilford.

MASTERSON, J. F. 1972. *The psychiatric dilemma of adolescence: A developmental approach.* Boston: Little, Brown.

———. 1976. *Psychotherapy of the borderline adult: A developmental approach.* New York: Brunner/Mazel.

MASTERSON, J. F., AND RINSLEY, D. 1975. The borderline syndrome: The role of the mother in the genesis and psychic structure of the borderline personality. *International Journal of Psychoanalysis, 56,* 163–77.

MEICHENBAUM, D., AND TURK, D. C. 1987. *Facilitating treatment adherence: A practitioner's guidebook.* New York: Plenum.

MILLER, L. J. 1990. The formal treatment contract in the inpatient management of borderline personality disorder. *Hospital & Community Psychiatry, 41*(9), 985–87.

ORLINSKY, D. E., AND HOWARD, K. I. 1986. Process and outcome in psychotherapy. In S. L. Garfield and A. E. Bergin (Eds.), *Handbook of psychotherapy and behavior change* (pp. 311–81). New York: John Wiley.

RACKER, H. 1957. The meanings and uses of countertransference. *Psychoanalytic Quarterly, 26,* 303–57.

References

REICH, W. 1949. *Character analysis,* 3rd ed. New York: Farrar, Straus and Cudahy.

SHEA, M. T., PILKONIS, P. A., BECKHAM, E., COLLINS, J. F., ELKIN, I., SOTSKY, S. M., AND DOCHERTY, J. P. 1990. Personality disorders and treatment outcome in the NIMH treatment of depression collaborative research program. *American Journal of Psychiatry, 27,* 143–53.

SKODOL, A., BUCKLEY, P., AND CHARLES, E. 1983. Is there a characteristic pattern to the treatment history of clinical outpatients with borderline patients? *Journal of Nervous and Mental Disease, 171*(7), 405–10.

STERBA, R. 1934. The fate of the ego in analytic therapy. *International Journal of Psychoanalysis, 15,* 117–26.

STONE, M. H. 1990. *The fate of borderline patients: Successful outcome and psychiatric practice.* New York: Guilford.

VOLKAN, V. D. 1987. *Six steps in the treatment of borderline personality organization.* Northvale, N.J.: Jason Aronson.

WALDINGER, R., AND GUNDERSON, J. 1984. Completed psychotherapies with borderline patients. *American Journal of Psychotherapy, 38*(2), 190–202.
———. 1987. *Effective psychotherapy with borderline patients: Case studies.* New York: Macmillan.

WINNICOTT, D. 1965. The theory of the parent-infant relationship. In D. Winnicott (Ed.), *The maturational process and the facilitating environment* (pp. 73–82). New York: International Universities Press.

YEOMANS, F. E., SELZER, M. A., AND CLARKIN, J. F. In press. Studying the treatment contract in intensive psychotherapy with borderline patients. *Psychiatry.*

Index